ALL HAIL
THE
MIGHTY STATE!

JUNE RAYFIELD WELCH

Texian Press ● **Waco, Texas** ● **1979**

Library of Congress Catalog Card No.
79-90784

ISBN 0-87244-048-6

Published by

Waco, Texas

For Kathryn, the Czech chick,
with gratitude and affection.

The Author

June Rayfield Welch has degrees from Texas Christian University, the University of Texas at Arlington, Texas Tech University and George Washington University. He practiced law prior to becoming Academic Dean of the University of Dallas where he is presently chairman of the Department of History. His books include: A FAMILY HISTORY (1965); THE TEXAS COURTHOUSE (1971); TEXAS: NEW PERSPECTIVES (1971); HISTORIC SITES OF TEXAS (1972); DAVE'S TUNE (1973); PEOPLE AND PLACES IN THE TEXAS PAST (1974); THE GLORY THAT WAS TEXAS (1975); AND HERE'S TO CHARLEY BOYD (1975); GOING GREAT IN THE LONE STAR STATE (1976); THE TEXAS GOVERNOR (1977); THE TEXAS SENATOR (1978).

Introduction

My formal education began during the depression at Benjamin Franklin Elementary School in north Gainesville, the poorest part of town and, we believed, the toughest. My father had gone to north school, too; one of his teachers, Miss Ethel Hood, had the second grade when I came along. She would call me "Frank" and I would say, "No ma'am, I'm June. Frank is my father."

Life was meager at north school in those years, but our needs were few and our tastes simple. We took special pride in the misuse of playground equipment. The half dozen seesaws were considered mainly as implements of destruction; one descended stiff-legged and bucked one's friend off the other end of the plank. The swings were utilized to hurl classmates into the air above the rocky playground where grass had not grown for five generations. (As the rider was given a final high shove the seat would be jerked out from under him.) The swings were convenient to Weaver Street and sometimes the inept were thrown into the northbound traffic.

At lunch and recess tops were played at a frenzied pace, as if the bottle caps we used for stakes were truly worth winning. (Across the street soft drink lids in mint condition collected in snowdrift-like heaps beside Milligan's Store.) The marble players had more character than the top spinners; more deliberate in their movements and possessed of a professional air, the great ones were marked by trousers which drooped beneath the weight of their winnings. Their thighs were mishapen by pockets stuffed with marbles.

The schoolyard teemed with red ants, ignored by all but those who devised primitive ant farms and a pupil who occasionally consumed one in the belief that it contained iodine and would prevent goiter. The barren yard also supported a large population of horned frogs, which were worthy of our attention. They fit well into the bib pocket of overalls and displayed tolerance, if not affection, for an owner. Although harmless, the toads appeared to be designed for combat and survival.

Texans had long admired the horned frog, which many believed could remain alive for a century if confined in an airless place. When the Eastland County courthouse was torn down, in 1928, and a live toad was removed from a cornerstone laid thirty years before, Texans were elated. Their belief in the hardihood of the horned toad was vindicated. Editor Boyce House, of the Eastland *Argus*, wrote stories about "Old Rip," whose nap had broken the record of twenty years held by Washington Irving's Rip Van Winkle. Newspapers throughout the nation made Rip famous and during an eastern tour he visited with Calvin Coolidge at the White House.

The horned frog's endurance was of special interest to West Texans, who had never experienced an oversupply of anything other than wind, dirt, heat and drought. Without water, food or air Rip had sustained himself. He was as tough as the early settlers, and some believed the horned frog more truly represented the state than the longhorn, an animal of courage and endurance but mainly a South Texas creature. Few Texans had seen longhorns, which were practically extinct, but there was an inexhaustible supply of toads.

Old Rip, who died a few months before the Great Depression began, was a symbol of that lean part of Texas in a lean time. He was the myth upon which Eastland based its claim to immortality. Embalmed and resting in a specially-built casket, he lay in state at the courthouse. In time Rip became the source of political tensions. Some felt Eastland's future was limited because of years of preoccupation with the desiccated lizard, but others could hardly think of the county separate from its most famous citizen.

Most of the stories in this volume concern Texans with Old Rip's kind of durability and strength. William Eastland, for whom that West Texas county was named, was a member of the Somervell and Mier expeditions. He drew the first black bean in the lottery at Hacienda Salado and was shot on March 25, 1843, by Santa Anna's order. José Navarro, a signer of the Texas Declaration of Independence, remained chained to the floor of his prison cell in Mexico long after the other Santa Fe Pioneers had been freed. Santa Anna tried to kill him through ill-treatment, but Navarro escaped and was serving in the Texas Senate when a county was named for him. (Its capital honored Navarro's Corsican father.) The husband of Navarro's niece, William Cooke, whose name my home county bears, was commander of the Santa Fe Expedition. After suffering terrible hardships Cooke and the other Pioneers were walked to Mexico and confined at Perote prison.

In addition to accounts of those dramatic demonstrations of physical courage and stamina, this book contains tales of men and women who had the kind of quiet, brave independence I saw in my parents and grandparents, which had to do with earning a living and hard work and frugality and perseverence. Noah T. Byars, as selfless as the Franciscans, expended his years in establishing Baptist churches. Uncle Charley Carlton, equally dedicated to his task and unconcerned by the price he paid, educated some Texans who simply became good citizens and others, such as Addison Clark, Randolph Clark and T. U. Taylor, who founded or shaped universities. Britisher W. J. Marsh, the organist for his own Catholic church and a Presbyterian congregation, played the organ for a Jewish synagogue every Saturday; he wrote the state song, "Texas, Our Texas."

Once more I am beholden to my good friends at the University of Dallas Library, the Texas Memorial Museum, and the Texas Archives, especially David Gracy, Chris La Plante and Jean Carefoot. Modesta Sprinkle, formerly of Monahans, Vonceil Muse, of Dallas, T. P. Fowler, of Loraine, good buddy Lynne Lutenbacher, of New Orleans, Betty Williams, of Denison, and Ernest Morrison, of Lubbock, dug up photographs and facts for me. Sister Ruth Quatman kept me in research materials; Sister Frances Marie Manning checked the manuscript; Raff Frano developed and printed most of my photographs, except for the time he was in Italy, when old friend Helen Bradley helped out. Nick and Joan Curtis designed the dust jacket, of which I am terribly proud. Ellen Fletcher, my neighbor, Anne Mary O'Reilly and Kolan Davis, my good student workers, and the folks at Davis Brothers Publishing Company, including Bob Davis, Bill Shirley, Mike Prim, Lane Price, Thomas Cochran, Edna Manry, and Cyndi Wendt, made the effort succeed. I thank my father and mother, Frank and Elzina Welch, for support and encouragement since the first of my books was in prospect.

June Rayfield Welch

September 3, 1979

Irving-on-the-Trinity, Texas

Table of Contents

ALL HAIL THE MIGHTY STATE!

JUNE RAYFIELD WELCH

The Settlement of Texas Began at Isleta, New Mexico

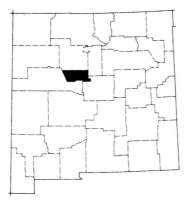

Isleta pueblo, twelve miles south of Albuquerque, is of special importance to Texans. Indians from Isleta fled south with Spanish refugees during the great rebellion of 1680; their village, Ysleta del Sur, now within the city limits of El Paso, is the oldest settlement in Texas. Of more consequence in the development of Texas, San Antonio de la Isleta was the New Mexico mission to which María de Agreda directed Jumano Indians to request that priests be sent to their country in Texas. That series of events, in which a Spanish nun apparently bilocated herself to the New World, stirred the Franciscans to prospect for souls in the big, empty land south and east of New Mexico and led to the founding of the first mission in Texas.

The mission of San Antonio was founded at Isleta about 1613. Father Fray Juan de Salas arrived there in 1622, built a fine church and monastery, and effected many conversions. The Franciscan Custodio brought thirty missionaries to New Mexico and made Isleta his headquarters about the time a delegation of fifty Jumano came asking for priests to teach their people, who then lived in the vicinity of present Tom Green County, Texas. Annually the Jumano had made the request, but never were there sufficient priests for the work at the pueblo. Now, in July of 1629, not only were there more Franciscans but an inquiry recently made by the Archbishop of Mexico City had aroused interest in the Indians living east of New Mexico. His Excellency wondered whether those nations demonstrated any knowledge of Christianity; if so, he wanted to know the source of their information.

Upon being questioned by the Franciscans, the Jumano declared that a lovely woman wearing a blue cloak had told them to seek missionaries in Isleta. When shown a painting of Mother Luisa de Carrión, the Indians agreed that the Woman in Blue was dressed in the same fashion but stated that she was much younger and was quite beautiful. The priests were appropriately excited, for the Archbishop's letter was occasioned by a young mother superior's claim that without leaving Spain she regularly visited New Mexico. Stimulated by the seeming bilocation of María de Agreda, Father de Salas and Father Fray Diego López, accompanied by three soldiers, went home with the Jumano delegation. After traveling about 300 miles they were greeted by twelve Jumano chiefs who explained that the woman in the blue dress had sent them to escort the Franciscans. Later the missionaries encountered a procession of some 2,000 Indians marching behind a cross made at the suggestion of the lady in the blue cloak. As the Franciscans preached to the Jumano, Indians from distant East Texas arrived, claiming that a beautiful lady who dressed in blue and often visited them had said priests were to be found among the Jumano. After laboring successfully in the Concho River country the priests returned to Isleta. In 1632 Father de Salas accompanied Father Fray Juan de Ortega to the land of the Jumano; Father Ortega remained with the Indians for about six months.

Because of interest generated by the story of the Woman in Blue, the Father President of the New Mexico Franciscans journeyed to Spain to investigate the claims of the nun. On April 30, 1631, Father Fray Alonso de Benavides interviewed the Mother María de Jesús, the 29-

The church of San Agustín de Isleta probably occupies the site of the original mission church founded in 1613. The enclosed courtyard once served as a cemetery.

year-old abbess of the Convent of the Immaculate Conception at Agreda, Spain. (She held that position until her death in 1665.) He reported that she was quite pretty and that she wore a brown sackcloth habit beneath a cloak of coarse blue cloth. She told him things one could have known only by spending time in New Mexico, and he declared himself completely satisfied with the truth of her claim that she, in some manner, had journeyed to the American Southwest about 500 times between 1620 and 1631. The Franciscans, believing the visits of the Woman in Blue constituted a divine mandate, begged to serve in Texas; as Carlos Castañeda put it, "the apostolic zeal of the faithful sons of Saint Francis had become an all-consuming passion."

In 1689, after finally discovering the ruins of La Salle's Fort St. Louis, in present Victoria County, Alonso De León and Father Fray Damian Massanet journeyed further north and east searching for French survivors. The chief of the Tejas Indians asked Father Massanet for blue baize in which to bury his mother. The color was of much importance, he stated, for a well-beloved lady who wore a blue cloak had come among his people many years ago and because of her the old people put great value upon blue burial clothing. Amazed by the Indian's knowledge of Christian practices—for he had never before seen a priest—Father Massanet promised to return. On June 1, 1690, De León and Father Massanet founded the Mission San Francisco de los Tejas and left there in East Texas three priests and three soldiers.

Almost a decade before this initial Spanish effort at settlement, the first permanent communities in Texas came into being as a result of the rebellion of the New Mexico pueblos. On August 10, 1680, led by a medicine man named Popé and infuriated by attempts to suppress their native religions, the Pueblo Indians cleared New Mexico of Spaniards. Twenty-one of the 32 Franciscans in the province were killed; it was the greatest single loss ever suffered by that order. About 2,800 Spaniards lived in haciendas along the Rio Grande and in Santa Fé, the only town. Many were descendants of the original settlers, who had arrived with Don Juan Oñate in 1598. Five or six hundred of the Spanish were killed, and the rest fled south to the Mission Guadalupe at the Pass of the North, in present Juarez, Mexico. Among the refugees were more than 300 Indians from Isleta pueblo, which had not revolted, and from the pueblos of Sevilleta, Alameda, Socorro and Senecú. Isletans founded the village which became Ysleta del Sur. Socorro del Sur was established a few months later.

Governor Antonio de Otermín led an expedition into New Mexico in 1681 but failed to recover the province. At Isleta he found cattle penned inside the ruins of the church. The convent had been burned. Most of the Isletans were living in other pueblos. Fearing that those remaining might lose their faith if left at Isleta and hoping to use them in Christianizing the Manso and others native to the Pass of the North, Otermín burned the pueblo and brought 385 Indians to live with their kinsmen at Ysleta. Many years later a change in the course of the river left Ysleta del Sur and Socorro del Sur on the American side of the Rio Grande, making them the oldest communities in Texas.

When the pueblo of Isleta, New Mexico, was refounded, about 1710, the church was renamed San Agustín de Isleta. The Pueblo Indians had always accommodated their old religion to that brought by the Franciscans. Trouble usually resulted from attempts to restore a balance when one party—medicine men or priests—feared that the other was becoming too strong.

The fortunes of the church waxed and waned. Sometimes affection was lavished upon the priests, as when the rumored transfer from Isleta of Father Felix Jouvet, in the middle of the nineteenth century, caused the oldest chief to beg him to stay and offer to ". . . get together all our people, large and small, counting more than 2,000, and if there is a single one who has any complaint to make against you, we will let you go." At other times relations between people

This photograph of Isleta's church, made by Dr. William A. Bell in 1867, is the earliest known.

and church were so poor as to justify complaints such as those of Father Fray Francisco Domínguez, who visited the pueblos in 1776:

> Even at the end of so many years since their reconquest, the specious title or name of neophytes is still applied to them. This is the reason their condition now is almost the same as it was in the beginning, for generally speaking they have preserved some very indecent, and perhaps superstitious, customs.

Most Indians did not bother to remember their Christian names, and "Their repugnance and resistance to most Christian acts is evident, for they perform the duties pertaining to the Church under compulsion, and there are usually many omissions." On July 8, 1776—when the ink was barely dry on the American Declaration of Independence—Father Domínguez reported that Isleta's population was 454 individuals, or 114 families, and inventoried the church property, which included an adobe altar and religious paintings done on buffalo skins.

Tensions between medicine men and priests continued through the years. The "old ways," as the native religions were styled, did not die out with the advent of the Europeans. The Pueblo Indians were accustomed to the threat posed by outsiders, the Apache, the Navajo, the Comanche and the nomads who preceded them. The Spaniards, the Mexicans, and the Americans were only the most recent foreigners to jeopardize the pueblo by their presence, and they, too, would disappear and would be succeeded by others. There would always be strangers; the people of the pueblos needed merely to outlast them.

Some of the outsiders' culture might be borrowed as long as the integrity of the community was not threatened. Dr. Elsie Clews Parsons, writing of Isleta nearly fifty years ago, noted that confession was made to medicine men as well as to priests and:

> Assimilation of Catholic ritual and ideology is unusually striking. A candle may be offered in the hills instead of a prayer feather; during irrigation ceremonial a cross blessed by the padre is placed at the river at the same time that prayer feathers are thrown into it; . . . ritual whipping is referred to as penance, and my informant compared the power of the . . . padre to change bread and wine into the host to the powers of the medicine men.

Indians of other tribes as well as non-Indians were excluded from important ceremonies. Isletans were to keep their customs secret from outsiders on penalty of being stricken by dread maladies. In 1927 a tribal council tried some Isletans on charges of furnishing material used in Charles Lummus' *Pueblo Indian Folktales*. One defendant was acquitted after showing that the book, published thirty years earlier, was based upon information supplied by an Indian long since dead. The other defendant had offended by winning a $50 prize in a contest to name a new Albuquerque movie theater. He suggested "Kimo," which meant mountain lion; not even Isletan words were to be revealed.

A prosecution based upon a book which was nearly a third of a century old suggests the absence of a sense of time or chronology some allege to be characteristic of Pueblo Indians. (A middle-aged man, upon being asked his father's birthday might answer 1967, or 1975, or 1950.) Such absence of an appreciation of sequence or duration—if true—might allow a people to consider the 400-year sojourn of men of European origin to be as ephemeral as the era of the Apache.

In June of 1955 Monsignor Fred Stadtmueller, a native of Germany, was assigned to the Isleta church. A veteran of fifteen years service in the pueblos, he had studied anthropology at the University of New Mexico and otherwise sought to understand the Indians. As attendance at San Agustín grew the Monsignor increased the number of Masses and began improving the church buildings and grounds. Evidently his early successes caused concern among the medicine societies, which may have been in decline. In the past most parishioners could be

The Isleta church, photographed by Ben Wittick in the late 19th century, was remodeled sometime after 1867. The bell was moved and two wooden towers were added.

expected at Mass except during Indian ceremonies; now tribal observances were moved to weekends, with consequent reductions in church attendance. Ceremonials became more numerous as old celebrations were revived. (Some said these revivals included the scalp dance condemned nearly two centuries earlier by Father Domínguez, who pointed out that the priests had always "been very zealous in their opposition to this scalp dance, but they have only received rebuffs, and so the fathers are unable to abolish this custom and many others . . . .")

The church then had a tin roof and wooden steeples. The Monsignor's plan to restore its earlier appearance provoked opposition, although the parish—not the pueblo, which owned the church—was paying for it. About the time of the renovation, in 1959, the medicine societies remodeled the kiva.

As the situation worsened Monsignor Stadtmueller scolded parishioners for missing Mass and they resented the changes he was making in the buildings and grounds. Prior to World War I the area in front of the church had been used for burials, but during the influenza epidemic the priest persuaded the governor to open a cemetery southwest of town. (The Indians blamed the German kaiser for the sickness.) After nearly half a century some church members still harbored resentments over the closing of the old cemetery, making any changes affecting the churchyard particularly sensitive.

The church and the front yard continued to be the principal sites for ceremonial dancing until Monsignor Stadtmueller covered part of the churchyard with concrete, planted the balance in cactus, and forbade use of the building for tribal celebrations. The Indians protested. Concrete was as much of an impediment as the cactus, for it kept dancers from contact with the earth. The Pueblo Indians believe that men originated in the earth. Their funeral preparations are made in a room having a dirt floor where the body is laid out, washed and dressed on the ground. Burial is without a coffin; should a coffin be used the lid is removed or propped open to permit contact with the earth.

Another complaint made against Monsignor Stadtmueller concerned the body buried beneath the altar. (Apparently the church has always occupied the same site; however, the pueblo officials have refused to permit excavations to test this assumption for fear that something might be found that would attract outsiders.) According to legend Father Padilla—called "the priest with the gold teeth"—a member of the Coronado expedition, rises from his grave every seven years. (In fact, Father Fray Juan de Padilla was killed about 1547 at Quivira. There is no reason why he would be buried at Isleta, for there was then no Spanish settlement in New Mexico and Isleta's first church would not be built for at least 65 years.) The priest interred beneath the church died about 1720 and was buried in a hollowed-out cottonwood log, which rose from time to time and cracked the dirt floor; probably water from the Rio Grande flows beneath the church in floodtime and floats the log. As part of his renovation the monsignor intended to install a wooden floor, but first he opened the grave, for many believed the body had not decomposed. In the presence of a pathologist and an anthropologist the top half of the log coffin was removed. The priest's forearms and hands were well-preserved. Remnants of a religious habit covered the skeleton and a metal box contained a note announcing that the body had been disinterred in 1893. A rumor that Monsignor Stadtmueller had poured a concrete slab to keep the priest from rising again infuriated some Isletans.

Finally, on June 20, 1965, the governor of Isleta and his son, the chief of police, came to Monsignor Stadtmueller's quarters after Mass, handcuffed him, drove him to the highway, let him out, and told him not to return. The old church was closed and boarded up. The

This photograph by Edward Kemp, probably dating from the 1920's, shows the addition of a pitched roof and more sophisticated towers to the church at Isleta Pueblo, New Mexico.

Archbishop of Albuquerque demanded an apology and acceptance of Monsignor Stadtmueller's return. Families divided over the controversy. The closing was a tragedy for those too old, ill, or poor to attend services elsewhere. There was no priest to conduct funerals. People got out of the habit of going to church, and children were not baptised. Some Isletans joined other denominations. After a few years priests from Ascension mission occasionally said Mass at Isleta but the church remained abandoned until 1974.

Three years after a pastor was again assigned to San Agustín Church, an event of much importance took place. On June 18, 1977, Edmund Paul Savilla, a full-blooded Indian, was ordained to the priesthood. Invitations had been sent to all the pueblos, and a thousand spectators saw the eagle dancers of Laguna pueblo and San Juan's buffalo dancers perform in the square. Father Savilla, of Isletan, Quechan and Onieda descent, wore moccasins and vestments decorated with Indian designs, and his hair was tied in a pueblo chongo: a short queue held by a brightly-colored cloth. Three hundred seventy-nine years after Don Juan Oñate opened New Mexico to Spanish settlement, Father Savilla became the first Pueblo Indian ordained by the Roman Catholic Church.

The interior of San Agustín Church at Isleta Pueblo, New Mexico as it appeared in 1978. Father Padilla's grave is beneath the pulpit on the left.

This cemetery at Isleta Pueblo, New Mexico has been used since the World War I influenza epidemic caused the priest to forbid further burials in the churchyard.

This painting, which hangs in the sanctuary of San Agustín de Isleta, is of unknown origin, but it was listed in the church inventory made by Father Fray Francisco Domínguez in 1776.

For Half a Century the Capital of Texas Was in Louisiana

At first the French were interested in Louisiana because they believed control of the Mississippi was necessary to the security of Canada. In addition, trade could be opened with Spain's colonies from Louisiana. In 1699 Pierre Le Moyne, Sieur de Iberville, brought his fleet to the mouth of the Mississippi after learning of British plans for occupying that position. He established a settlement at Biloxi and later built a fort which was commanded by his brother, Jean Baptiste Le Moyne, Sieur de Bienville, and Louis Juchereau St. Denis. Bienville founded New Orleans in 1718, and St. Denis would precipitate a French scare that would cause Spain to try to settle Texas.

On September 12, 1712, Louis XIV gave Antoine Crozat a fifteen-year monopoly of the trade of Louisiana, and Crozat appointed Governor de la Mothe Cadillac to run the colony. Because there were only about 700 colonists in all of Louisiana, trade with Spain's possessions was essential to the success of the venture. In 1717 Crozat relinquished the colony after having been unable to develop substantial commerce with the Spanish colonies.

In the meantime Natchitoches, the oldest permanent settlement in present Louisiana, had been founded by St. Denis. Offering as his excuse for sanctioning trespass on Spanish soil a letter from Father Fray Francisco Hidalgo requesting aid to his Tejas mission, Governor Cadillac sent St. Denis into Texas with a stock of trade goods. (By then Father Hidalgo had given up and returned to Mexico, for his letter was two and a half years old when Cadillac received it.) St. Denis, in 1714, built storehouses for his merchandise at the Natchitoches Indian Village on Red River, and after posting guards he went on to Texas. His trade with the Hasinai flourished, making it necessary for St. Denis to obtain a new stock of goods.

In the fall of 1714 St. Denis walked across Texas. His appearance at the presidio of San Juan Bautista on the Rio Grande shocked the Spaniards. Not only had a foreigner entered Texas in violation of Spanish law, but he, his three French companions, and three Indian guides had traversed the entire province without detection, demonstrating how very inadequate were Spain's defenses. St. Denis was arrested and sent to Mexico for an interview with the viceroy, who decided to reoccupy Texas.

In 1716 Domingo Ramón led an expedition into Texas to found missions and presidios which would block any French advance. Ramón's guide was the same St. Denis whose presence had caused the alarm. Ramón reestablished the Mission Nuestra Padre San Francisco de los Tejas on the Neches River four leagues east of the original location; Father Hidalgo, after many years of hoping for such an opportunity, was the pastor. A presidio was built a short distance away. After the founding of Mission La Purísima Concepción, the Mission Nuestra Señora de Guadalupe, and the Mission San José, Ramón continued on to the French outpost of Natchitoches. There he found two Frenchmen on an island, which had a house and a stockade, and Father Fray Antonio Margil de Jesús delivered the first Mass ever celebrated at Natchitoches.

Ramón decided to establish a mission near Natchitoches. Returning along the road they

On this hill near present Robeline, Louisiana, stood the presidio Los Adaes, which functioned as the capital of Texas for 50 years.

had followed, the Spanish halted at the village of the Adaes, about fifteen miles away. There Father Margil founded the Mission San Miguel de Linares. Located near present Robeline, fifteen miles west of Red River, San Miguel was the only Spanish mission in what is now Louisiana. Ramón continued westward, establishing the Mission Nuestra Señora de los Dolores de los Ais, with Father Margil in charge. All six missions were founded in 1716.

Among the consequences of the declaration of war by France against Spain in January, 1719, was the French seizure of Pensacola and the order by Bienville, the governor of Louisiana, for the expulsion of the Spanish from San Miguel de los Adaes. In June the Natchitoches commander M. Blondel and his invading army of seven soldiers discovered at Los Adaes only a lay brother and one soldier (always described as ragged by historians.) The missionaries were away. Blondel was about to depart with his two prisoners of war and the furnishings of the church when the mission flock of chickens became excited. (The French may have been taking them into custody also.) The noise and the flapping of their wings inspired Blondel's horse into throwing him. In the resulting confusion the lay brother escaped and warned the other missions that 100 French soldiers were en route from Mobile. The Spanish force numbered no more than 25 untrained soldiers, some with neither horse nor weapon. The Spaniards quickly abandoned the East Texas missions as well as Los Adaes.

The war with France had ended by the time the Spanish returned to East Texas. The Marquis of San Miguel de Aguayo, Joseph Azlor Virto de Vera, had been made governor of Coahuila and Texas. His expedition, consisting of about 500 men, 5,000 horses and 800 mules, entered Texas in March of 1721. Aguayo stopped at San Antonio de Valero, which had been founded in 1718, and visited the mission Father Antonio Margil had opened in 1720, the Mission San José y San Miguel de Aguayo.

From San Antonio the marquis journeyed eastward and began reestablishing missions. St. Denis, the commander at Natchitoches, tried to talk Aguayo out of reoccupying San Miguel de los Adaes. By late August, 1721, the expedition was at Los Adaes, which the Indians had deserted after Frenchmen had abducted some women and children. Aguayo ordered the new Mission San Miguel reestablished not far from the presidio he was building, but Father Margil was to postpone erecting the necessary buildings until the Indians congregated in the spring.

The Presidio Nuestra Señora del Pilar was located by Aguayo on a hilltop half a league from the original mission, of which not a trace remained. The log fortification was built in the shape of a hexagon and stockaded. It had three bastions, on each of which two brass cannons were mounted, and commanded the countryside below, including the water supply. A well was to be dug within the fort, and early plans called for reinforcement of the stockade with adobe walls since "there is no stone available, not even of the smallest kind." The presidio had accomodations for the Franciscans, and its chapel was in use well before the mission was built. Of the hundred men in the garrison, 28 were married and their families lived nearby. The town which developed had a population of about 500.

Aguayo left Don Fernando Pérez de Almazán in command of Texas. He had informed the viceroy that distances were too great for a single governor and recommended separating Texas from Coahuila. The viceroy concurred; Almazán became the governor in 1722, and for the next half century Adaes presidio was the capital of Texas.

Although the object in establishing the presidio was to keep the French out of Spanish territory and to enforce the laws forbidding trade with foreigners, traffic was heavy between Natchitoches and Adaes, as might be expected of two lonely, European wilderness outposts. Furthermore, the Spaniards depended upon Natchitoches for food, since they had no crops.

This marker on the main street of Natchitoches, Louisiana, is a reminder of the founding of the town by St. Denis, which resulted in the establishment of Los Adaes by Spaniards seeking to halt French expansion.

(St. Denis had warned Aguayo against the poor climate and soil of Adaes.) Commerce with the French was a constant problem, for Spaniards could not trade legally with outsiders. In 1730 the viceroy ordered the presidio relocated in an area capable of cultivation, but the governor replied that he could find no better land between Red River and the Sabine. The viceroy then modified the trade prohibitions to allow necessary food supplies to be brought from Natchitoches. Later officials had to compromise in similar fashion, for they did not want to move the fort west of the Sabine nor did they wish to haul supplies from Mexico. The legal commerce with Louisiana in beans and corn served to cover traffic in all manner of contraband.

The commanders of the outposts were usually on good terms. Once the governor of Adaes sent troops to assist St. Denis when Natchez Indians put Natchitoches under seige. In 1735, St. Denis moved his fort from the island to the western bank of Red River, where a settlement had grown up; the Spanish commander protested but took no further action. The Franciscans said Mass in Natchitoches, which had no regularly assigned priest until 1729. Marriages occurred between residents of the two settlements, and the funeral of St. Denis, in June of 1744, was attended by the Spanish governor.

The French got along well with the Indians of East Texas as well as those of Louisiana. Spanish law did not permit guns and ammunition to be sold to Indians, a prohibition which stimulated trade and strengthened friendships between French traders and the Caddo, Hasinai and other Texas nations.

The governor at Adaes was the highest civil and military official of the province of Texas; fifteen men served between 1722 and 1772, when San Antonio became the capital. An extant drawing shows the governor's residence, built about 1735, with a hipped roof and a 54-foot gallery across the front. In 1763, the year France eliminated the need for a border post by ceding Louisiana to Spain, a Frenchman gave this description of the Spanish village:

> The settlement of Adaes consists of about forty miserable houses, constructed with stakes driven into the ground. It is situated on the declivity of a hill, the top of which, formed into a square, and enclosed with palisadoes, such as I saw at Natchitoches, served as a kind of fortress to the village . . . . The houses are scattered about the west side of the fort; and a little valley, lying in the same quarter separates the village from a considerable eminence on which stands a church and a convent of Franciscans.

The Marquis de Rubí, after his 1767 inspection tour, recommended that Spain abandon everything north and east of Bexar and La Bahía de Espíritu Santo. At Adaes the 61 soldiers were idle, since the Indians gave no trouble. The garrison was composed partly of fugitives from justice. Although the presidio was supposed to own 228 horses, only 117 were actually there: 25 horses of good quality, 43 fairly valuable animals, and 49 useless nags. Only two carbines were in good condition and the seven swords were of no value. Many soldiers had no mounts; some owned only parts of a uniform and appeared at formal review bareheaded, shoeless, and wearing dirty, ragged shirts. Ill-fed and housed, the troops were in no condition for service.

At the mission lived two priests—in dire need—but no neophytes. There were no crops. Not only did food have to be imported but hay was hauled from ten leagues away. The Indians would not live at the mission; those attracted to Christianity preferred to stay at the presidio. Mission records reflected that 103 baptisms had occurred, but at the presidio chapel 256 baptisms, 64 marriages and 116 funerals had taken place and Natchitoches, with no resident priest, had recorded twenty baptisms, thirteen marriages and fifteen funerals.

The location of the boundary was always in question. French and Spanish officials made temporary agreements which had no legal force but later influenced the permanent settlement. In 1724 Governor Sandoval and the French commander at Natchitoches arbitrarily established the Arroyo Hondo—which had long been so regarded—as the dividing line.

In 1773 the three East Texas missions and the one at Adaes were ordered suppressed. Los Adaes presidio was to be abandoned and the settlers were to move to San Antonio. The governor, the Baron de Ripperdá, was to effect the relocation of missionaries, troops and settlers. He estimated the Adaes population at 500, a figure he may have exaggerated because of reluctance to uproot the settlers, who did not want to leave their homes. (References to fields of corn and anticipated rich harvests make one skeptical of earlier reports of the soil's unproductivity issued while officials were justifying the trade between Adaes and Natchitoches.)

To avoid the move to San Antonio many fled to Natchitoches or took up residence among the Indians. The people, given no opportunity to harvest crops or to plan for the move, began their hard journey to San Antonio on June 25, 1773. A dozen women and children died on the road. The others reached Bexar on September 26.

As soon as Adaes was evacuated Indians and Frenchmen from Natchitoches looted the buildings and dug up possessions the owners had hoped to conceal until they could return for them. Some Adaes residents who had eluded the governor and about three dozen escapees from the San Antonio-bound column appropriated whatever remained of the abandoned property.

At San Antonio the uprooted people asked permission to move to Ais, present San Augustine. Instead Antonio Gil Ybarbo, their leader, was given authority to relocate them in East Texas no nearer Natchitoches than 100 leagues. Ais was within the prohibited area. At the Trinity River Ybarbo founded the town of Nuestra Señora del Pilar de Bucareli, which had a population of 347 in 1777. Sickness, Comanche troubles, and the flooding of the townsite doomed Bucareli and in 1779 Ybarbo led his people to the old Nacogdoche Indian village and, moving them into the deserted mission buildings, he founded modern Nacogdoches.

Soon after they learned of the Louisiana Purchase the Spaniards sent troops to Adaes. In February of 1806 Captain Edward Turner, with sixty American soldiers, forced the Spanish to withdraw beyond the Sabine. In this manner a neutral ground was created; the Americans at Natchitoches agreed not to advance beyond the Arroyo Hondo if the Spanish remained west of the Sabine.

J. Fair Hardin, in his fine work on Adaes, quoted the Reverend Timothy Flint's description of the village in 1824:

> It is a curious collection of great, upright log houses, plastered with mud, and having an appearance very different from a French village of the same character. The church was a mean log building, with four bells, some of them cracked, and pictures of saints, that, from their horrible ugliness, might have been taken for caricatures.

The residents spoke Spanish and made tortillas; in modern times their descendants lived about two miles from Adaes at Spanish Lake, Hardin reported. "There one may hear Spanish spoken as it was spoken in 1721, more than two centuries ago when their ancestors came . . . from old Mexico." When the Texas and Pacific came through in 1882 the town of Robeline was founded beside the right-of-way and Adaes was abandoned. In 1931 the Adaes presidio site was sold by Joe Welch (whose family acquired it prior to Texas annexation) to the Daughters of American Colonists, who donated the 9.15 acres to Natchitoches Parish.

Zachary Taylor Founded Fort Jesup

France and Spain never agreed upon the boundary separating Louisiana from Texas, and the question still was not resolved on October 1, 1800, when Spain ceded Louisiana to France "with the same extent that it had when France possessed it." The limits remained undetermined as the United States bought the Louisiana Territory from France in 1803.

It was not until April, 1805, that an American army officer relieved the Spanish garrison at Natchitoches by assuming command. (After receiving Louisiana from Spain, the French had never gotten around to sending troops to take possession.) Spain, upset by Napoleon's sale of Louisiana and unwilling to part with any claims she might have, reoccupied Adaes. Captain Moses Porter sent an officer and sixty men from Natchitoches who persuaded the 21 Spaniards to withdraw beyond the Sabine.

In 1806 Colonel Simón de Herrera led an army of more than 1,000 Spanish soldiers across the Sabine. At the same time United States Army Colonel Thomas Cushing was at Natchitoches with artillery and regular troops and Governor William C. C. Claiborne had arrived with militia at nearby Fort Claiborne. General James Wilkinson was also on the scene, talking of an attack. (During this time Wilkinson, the ranking American general, was intriguing with Aaron Burr, the Spaniards, and just about everyone else.)

On November 4, 1806, Wilkinson and Herrera agreed that the Americans would halt east of the Arroyo Hondo, a creek four miles west of Natchitoches, and the Spanish would remain west of the Sabine until their nations effected a final boundary settlement.

In that fashion the neutral ground was created, and into that no-man's land, thirty miles across, swarmed the country's worst cutthroats. There, free from prosecution for past and future offenses, they could prey on travelers following the Camino Real, or San Antonio Road, which extended from Natchitoches across Texas to the Rio Grande.

The Treaty of Washington, in 1819, established the boundary at the Sabine, giving the United States ownership of the neutral ground and all its problems. The formal transfer was effected on July 17, 1821, and Lieutenant Colonel Zachary Taylor, President James Madison's second cousin, was ordered to guard the new border, maintain peace among the Indians, and protect traffic over the San Antonio Road from denizens of the "Free State of Sabine," as local cynics termed the neutral ground. With four companies of infantry Taylor reached Natchitoches in November and wintered twelve miles farther west at a campsite he named Fort Selden.

A permanent location on the Camino Real at the highest point between Red River and the Sabine, was selected by Taylor and his superior, General Edmund P. Gaines. The site, nine miles west of Los Adaes, was midway between Natchitoches and the Sabine River. Named for Taylor's good friend, General Thomas Jesup, the reservation originally covered one square mile. The construction of Cantonment Jesup began in early 1822. Taylor's service was brief; his successors in command of the fort included Colonel James B. Many, Brigadier General Henry Leavenworth, and Colonel David Twiggs.

Fort Jesup was the main factor in development of the area. The post afforded protection for those who used the Camino Real; it stimulated settlement and was the center of the local

Lieutenant Colonel Zachary Taylor established Fort Jesup in 1822, naming the Louisiana post for his good friend General Thomas Jesup. Taylor and Jesup had a falling out later over the service given his army at Corpus Christi by quartermaster general Jesup.

21

society and economy. Initially the garrison occupied pine log cabins set on stone foundations. Building materials were plentiful, as was good drinking water. Roads were cut through the forests to provide connections with forts Claiborne and Selden, in Louisiana, and Towson, in the Indian Territory. (Towson and Jesup were then the westernmost posts of the United States Army.)

The reservation was expanded to include all land within three miles of the flagpole, and in Fort Jesup's prime 82 buildings were in use. The regimental band played for dances, and horse races were held regularly. Many immigrants, including Stephen F. Austin, David Crockett, and Jim Bowie, stopped at the fort on the way to Texas. Colonel William F. Gray, Texas-bound in January of 1836, considered Jesup a "pleasant place . . . . Very healthy . . . . The gardens are very fine, abundance of fine vegetables, flowers now in bloom, peach trees in bloom . . . ."He enjoyed the band music and attended a party where he played backgammon.

As Texas statehood became imminent the United States, uneasy over Mexico's long-standing threat to regard annexation as an act of aggression, moved troops to Fort Jesup. In April, 1844, Brevet Brigadier General Zachary Taylor, 59 years old, became commander of the First Department of the Army, with headquarters at Fort Jesup. According to Holman Hamilton he was told:

> You will take prompt measures . . . to put yourself in communication with the President of Texas, in order to inform him of your present position and force, and to learn and to transmit to this office (all confidentially) whether any and what external dangers threaten that Government or its people.

In June the army consisted of seven companies of the Second Dragoons, eight of the Third Infantry, and eight companies of the Fourth Infantry—about 1,000 effective soldiers—stationed at Jesup and nearby camps Salubrity and Wilkins. (Colonel Vose, the superannuated commander of the Fourth, dropped dead while drilling his troops.) Lt. U. S. Grant's regiment was at Camp Salubrity, about three miles from Natchitoches on a ridge too high for mosquitoes. Grant, a critic of Texas statehood, would have preferred to teach mathematics at West Point as he had intended; even so, Grant enjoyed the horse races and the hospitality of planters living along Red River.

Elected on the slogan of "Polk, Dallas, Texas, and Oregon," James K. Polk became president in March of 1845, soon after Congress invited Texas into the Union. On May 28 Taylor was instructed by the Secretary of War:

> So soon as the Texas Congress shall have given its consent to annexation, and a convention shall assemble and accept the terms offered in the resolution of Congress, Texas will then be regarded by the executive government here as so far a part of the United States as to be entitled . . . to defense from foreign invasion and Indian incursions. The troops under your command will be placed and kept in readiness to perform that duty.

In June he was ordered to move the "Army of Observation" to a port from which it could proceed to the Rio Grande upon ratification by Texas. Taylor sent the infantry regiments to New Orleans by steamboat. After the Texans accepted statehood, on July 4, 1845, General David Twiggs' dragoons departed for San Antonio over the Camino Real. On July 23 Taylor and his foot-soldiers sailed from New Orleans for Corpus Christi.

The annexation of Texas having moved the international boundary 800 miles to the Rio Grande, Fort Jesup was no longer needed. The "Cradle of the Mexican War" was closed in 1845 and left to caretakers. Part of the reservation was subdivided and sold in 1849. Fort Jesup Masonic Institute operated on the site in the 1890's. The town which grew up at the old post died long ago. Only a log kitchen remains of Fort Jesup's buildings; it was restored about 1930. A replica of a residence for officers presently serves as a museum.

For a quarter of a century Fort Jesup, Louisiana, and Fort Towson, in the Indian Territory, were the westernmost outposts of the United States. At Fort Jesup troops gathered by Zachary Taylor were trained for service in case of war with Mexico over Texas annexation. This replica of an officers quarters serves as a museum.

T. J. Chambers Owned The Capitol Grounds

Thomas Jefferson Chambers, the youngest of twenty children, was born in Orange County, Virginia, on April 13, 1802. After his father's death the Chambers family moved to Kentucky. Licensed as an attorney in Kentucky, Chambers practiced in Alabama before going to Mexico. In 1829 he came to Texas as Surveyor-General.

While teaching English in Mexico City, Chambers acquired Mexican citizenship, and he was admitted to the practice of law in 1834. For helping to establish a judicial circuit in Texas he was appointed Assessor General, a position he described as "an advisory office . . . controlling all the inferior judges of the State," but illness forced him to resign in May of 1834. A few weeks thereafter the governor made Chambers the Superior Judge of Texas, but because of controversies such as the dispute between Monclova and Saltillo over location of the capitol, the legislature never confirmed him. In the meantime he had undertaken to perform his duties; Chambers asked the alcaldes to hold elections for constables and sheriffs and to provide machinery for jury selection, but he received little cooperation. He wrote a Code of Practice which consisted of about 200 articles designed to guide the administration of justice, but apparently the legislature never gave its approval.

In 1835 Chambers agreed to payment of his salary—$3,000 a year—in land since the Coahuila y Texas treasury was short of funds. He accepted fifteen leagues, which was less than the amount due, for as a Mexican citizen he could purchase land from the public domain at 4¢ an acre. (A square league contained 4,428.4 acres.) He also received grants of five leagues for his services as Surveyor-General. Apparently Chambers purchased additional tracts, because altogether he owned or was owed by the government, 30 leagues—132,852 acres. On June 20, 1835, eight leagues "on the eastern margin of the Colorado River near the foot of the mountains" were patented to Chambers; this parcel included the site of present Austin. His holdings included the Chambers County grant where Anahuac is situated.

Always engaged in controversy, Chambers regarded Stephen F. Austin as a weakling who was used by his friends, and Sam Houston declared that something fundamental was lacking in a man who signed himself "T. Jefferson Chambers." In her excellent thesis Llerena Friend stated:

> He did have considerable egotism and an unfailing ability to make enemies. People seemed unable to trust him, believed him vascillating, an opportunist ready to support whatever group happened to be in power and could afford him the most advancement.

As the drift toward revolution accelerated Chambers aspired to leadership, although more than once he changed his mind about the proper course for Texas. Even after the fighting began Chambers belonged to the peace party, but by the end of October, 1835, he had declared for revolution. He offered to solicit soldiers and arms in the United States and to cover expenses by advancing $10,000 as a loan and pledging the credit of Texas for the balance. The General Council, on January 7, 1836, created an "Army of Reserve" under Chambers' command. He recruited and raised funds in Kentucky until March, 1837. As a major general he believed that only Sam Houston ranked him, a claim the Republic did not acknowldege.

By virtue of his services to Mexico Thomas Jefferson Chambers received huge land grants in Texas. The City of Austin occupies some of his land.

(Attorney General Peter Grayson considered Chambers "the most undeserving of mortals." The provisional government of a Mexican state had commissioned him, but Texas was not part of Mexico after March 2, 1836.)

Chambers never commanded troops, but his nephew reported that he recruited and equipped 1,915 Kentuckians, who did not reach Texas until after the San Jacinto victory. The cannons he bought at Pittsburgh were labeled "Presented to the Republic of Texas by Major General T. J. Chambers." Two of the six flank the entrance to the capitol. The Republic reimbursed Chambers $23,621.00 for funds he had borrowed to recruit and transport soldiers, but the currency was too badly depreciated to cover the debts. Years passed before he was able to pay the notes and free his land from mortgages.

The Congress of the Republic, on January 4, 1839, voted to move the capital. Commissioners selected the Austin site which then accommodated the hamlet of Waterloo, and Congress appropriated $15,000 to purchase the 5,004-acre tract. Chambers was not made a party to the condemnation suit and was surprised when he learned that the seat of government was to occupy his land. After Congress ordered the defendants paid and Chambers' claim was ignored, on February 7, 1840, he filed his instruments of title in the General Land Office.

Since Chambers was not a defendant in the suit his ownership was not affected. When he sued to eject Josiah Fisk and 45 others who were living on the grant, the court at Georgetown held against him. On appeal, in 1858, Supreme Court Justice Oran Roberts upheld his title to the Colorado grant, including the Austin townsite.

At 48, Chambers married 18-year-old Abbie Chubb. They lived at Chambersia, his Anahuac home. Their daughters, Kate and Stella, were born in 1852 and 1864. Chambers was defeated by Peter Bell for governor in 1851. Two years later he lost to E. M. Pease. In 1861 Francis Lubbock defeated him, and in 1863 he lost to Pendleton Murrah. Chambers County, created in 1858, was named for him.

Near the end of the Civil War, Chambersia was lost through suits for debt of which Chambers had no personal knowledge, having been served by publication. A man named McDonald occupied the home; Chambers rode past regularly, although once someone shot at him. One day Chambers noticed that the house was empty and took possession. McDonald found Chambers' mule tied at the gate when he returned; he called for Chambers to come out. As Martha Stormont told it:

> Suspecting treachery he loaded his gun, a double-barreled one, one barrel a rifle and the other a shotgun. With his foot against the door he carefully opened it and there stood McDonald and his companion with cocked guns. As Chambers stepped out, they raised their guns, but he was too quick for them. He killed McDonald with one barrel and desperately wounded the other man with the second barrel.

Title was cleared in the courts and Chambers moved back into Chambersia, but on a March evening in 1865:

> He was sitting in his library with his back to an open window with his little six-month-old daughter, Stella, on his knee. A shot rang out. General Chambers slowly slumped forward and would have fallen to the floor had not his wife caught him. He never spoke after that, and in a few minutes, he was dead.

The killer was never caught.

Mrs. Chambers married Cyrus Saladee and moved to Connecticutt. Kate married Fred Sturgis; widowed, she taught in Galveston for nearly forty years. Stella married Donald

Thomas Jefferson Chambers was shot and killed at his home, Chambersia, in Anahuac, Chambers County.

MacGregor. After many attempts to obtain payment for the Capitol grounds—the heirs had agreed to relinquish their interest in the balance of the Austin townsite—in 1925 the state paid $20,000, and the Chambers daughters executed a warranty deed to the 25 acres occupied by the Texas capitol.

Chambers was authorized to solicit funds and soldiers for the Texas Revolution. He bought six cannons in the United States; these two, flanking the entrance of the Texas Capitol, bear the inscriptions: "Presented to the Republic by Major General T. J. Chambers in 1836" and "This gun was used during the Texas Revolution and in the Civil War. For many years it was mounted in front of the State, War and Navy Building, Washington, D.C. Through the efforts of Honorable W. C. Day, Superintendent of Public Buildings and Grounds and Honorable A. S. Burleson it was returned to Texas in 1910."

Jack Hays Was The Border Guardian

John Coffee Hays was born January 28, 1817, in Tennessee. His father, Harmon Hays, a nephew of Rachel Donelson Jackson, had served under General John Coffee in the Creek War. At fifteen John Hays joined a surveying party in Mississippi; at nineteen, learning of the Alamo's fall, he came to Texas. Reaching Nacogdoches shortly before the battle of San Jacinto, Hays enlisted in the army and helped bury victims of the Goliad massacre.

At San Antonio that December, Hays joined Deaf Smith's Ranger company; he was soon promoted to sergeant, but the pay was low and irregular and he surveyed when his duties permitted. Hundreds of men with land certificates sought surveyors with knowledge of the frontier to locate their claims. Indian fights were common near San Antonio; within a year a hundred young men in search of land or adventure were killed by Indians and badmen.

Hays, a Ranger captain at 23, was also the elected Bexar County surveyor. His Rangers furnished San Antonio's only defense, and they fought many battles. The Indians called him "Devil Jack." Quoting John Caperton (after whom Hays named his son) James Greer wrote: "About half of the Rangers were killed off every year, and their places were supplied by new men. The lives of those who went into the service were not considered good for more than a year or two."

The Rangers were the first to appreciate fully the advantages of Samuel Colt's revolving pistols; Hays wore two five-shooters in his 1841 battle at the Enchanted Rock. Camped nearby he had climbed the 1,825-foot peak alone since none of his men wanted to make the effort. Indians regarded the great granite dome as a place of strong medicine, perhaps because of sounds the rock allegedly made on cool evenings following hot days. While descending the mountain Hays encountered about twenty Comanche and scrambled back to the summit where a crater-like depression afforded him cover. He had no way to reload his rifle and pistols. After two hours of fighting the Indians charged. Hays had resorted to using the rifle as a club when the Rangers attacked some Indians climbing the rock and the war party retreated. Hays was not hurt, although several Indians were dead.

After Mexican generals Vasquez and Woll had captured San Antonio, Hays' Rangers accompanied the Somervell expedition to the Rio Grande; they returned with the main column as 300 volunteers broke away, invaded Mexico, were captured in Mier, and wound up in Mexican prisons.

Ranger James Nichols left a good description of the training Hays gave his men; the company was camped at one of the missions south of San Antonio in 1843. Those not on patrol were kept busy improving their skills as horsemen and marksmen. "We put up a post about the size of a common man, then put up another about 40 yards farther on. We would run our horses full speed and discharge our rifles at the first post, draw our pistols and fire at the second." They practiced Comanche trick riding, and after three or four months, Nichols states, using spellings more efficacious than correct;

> we became so purfect that we would run our horses half or full speede and pick
> up a hat, a coat, a blanket, or rope, or even a silver dollar, stand up in the saddle,

John Coffee Hays, the great Ranger captain, became the first sheriff of San Francisco County, California, and the founder of Oakland.

throw ourselves on the side of our horses with only a foot and a hand to be seen, and shoot our pistols under the horses neck . . . .

When Zachary Taylor's army reached Corpus Christi in 1845, four Ranger companies commanded by Jack Hays were mustered into federal service and assigned the missions of Indian defense and reconnaissance against the Mexicans. In June of 1846 Hays was elected colonel of the First Regiment, Texas Mounted Rifles, an outfit composed of about 700 frontiersmen, Indian fighters, and former Rangers such as Lieutenant Colonel Samuel Walker, Major Michael Chevaille, and Captain Ben McCulloch. After the battle of Monterey Hays brought his men back to Texas to be discharged.

Not long after his marriage to Susan Calvert, in 1847, Hays' second regiment was on the way to Mexico. It was turned back because the term of enlistment of the men was only six months. After raising a regiment of men enlisted for a year Hays left part in Texas for frontier service under Colonel Peter Bell and took the rest to Mexico. Hays' men went to great lengths to prove by their dress that they were not soldiers. Greer quoted a New Orleans *Picayune* description of "Los Diablos Tejanos" as they entered Mexico City:

> Dressed as Rangers always are, in anything that comes to hand—some with blankets wrapped around them, and some in their shirt sleeves—but all well mounted and well armed, they presented a sight never before seen in the streets of Mexico, and the usually noisy Léperos were as still as death—while they were passing. The gallant Jack Hays appeared to be the object of particular interest, and the better informed class of Mexicans were particularly anxious to have pointed out to them the man whose name has been the terror of their nation for the past twelve years.

Hays was one of the escort assigned to see former president Santa Anna out of Mexico as he departed for Venezuelan exile in April of 1848. Arriving in Powder Horn, Texas after the war, Hays wore the Mexican dictator's coat, which was valued at $1,000 and weighed fifteen pounds because of its gold ornaments. A few weeks earlier Hays County had been named for him.

Hays organized an expedition to lay out a road from San Antonio, by way of El Paso, to Chihuahua, hoping to divert some of the heavy Santa Fé trade. Samuel Maverick was among the three dozen who left Bexar with him on August 27, 1848. They passed through Fredericksburg and met Captain Samuel Highsmith and about 35 others—including a Delaware Indian interpreter—on the Llano River. After severe hardships the party reached Presidio del Norte—Ojinaga—and the ranch of Benjamin Leaton, who was then building Fort Leaton. They were within 150 miles of El Paso, but having expended too much time and stamina they turned back. Following a different route, the party arrived in San Antonio on December 10 after an absence of 106 days and a journey of 1,300 miles. They were in terrible physical condition. Highsmith died soon thereafter. They had stopped short of El Paso, but the expedition was not a failure; Hays had reached Presidio del Norte, from which a road led to Chihuahua, with the consequence that some of the Santa Fé trade was channeled to Texas.

In 1849 Hays was appointed Indian agent for the Gila River country at $400 per annum. Heading west to commence his duties, Hays travelled near the road-building company of Army Captain Joseph E. Johnston and the escort of Major Jefferson Van Horn. Johnston was preparing a road to Paso del Norte. The military expedition, made up of six infantry companies, 275 wagons, and 2,500 animals, was accompanied by 200 California immigrants and departed on June 3. Hays' party of about forty men followed a few days later; on September 10 they stopped at the ranch of Benjamin Coontz on the site of present El Paso. At the Gila River, Hays decided against trying to work with the Apache. After resigning his agency he went on to California.

At San Francisco, which had grown from 25,000 to 40,000 in a few months, Hays was elected sheriff in April of 1850. Mrs. Hays arrived that December. Sheriff Hays resigned in 1853 to become the Surveyor General of California. After founding Oakland, in 1858 he tried to get the state capitol moved there. Hays died April 21, 1883, near Piedmont, California.

The Santa Fe Pioneers Were Taken Captive

In November of 1840 President M. B. Lamar asked the Texas Congress to finance an expedition which would open direct trade with Santa Fé. When no appropriation was made, Lamar simply ordered disbursements from the public treasury amounting to about $90,000. William G. Cooke, 33 years old, was the commander of the expedition. His fellow commissioners were José Antonio Navarro, Dr. Richard Brenham, and Willian G. Dryden, a Santa Fé resident who had reported to Lamar that Governor Manuel Armijo and the people of New Mexico were well-disposed toward Texas. George Van Ness was appointed secretary to the commissioners. The commissioners, merchants and goods would be escorted by volunteers commanded by Brevet Brigadier General Hugh McLeod, a 27-year-old West Point graduate. McLeod later married the president's cousin, Rebecca Lamar. The adjutant, Major George Thomas Howard, was an experienced frontiersman.

The commissioners carried copies of a Lamar proclamation stating that Texas' western boundary was the Rio Grande and hailing residents of eastern New Mexico as fellow citizens of the Republic. The commissioners were to take charge of the government at Santa Fé; however, should there be opposition they were to establish trade connections and return home. Santa Fé was invited to send three delegates to the next Texas Congress.

The inauguration of commercial relations with Santa Fé would have been of enormous benefit to the bankrupt Republic. Annually goods worth from three to twenty million dollars were hauled over the trail that William Becknell had opened between Santa Fé and Missouri in 1822. Manufactures from the East were bartered in Santa Fé for Mexican pelts, gold and silver. The American goods were taken into northern Mexico, from whence the hides and metals came. Proponents of the Santa Fé Expedition pointed out that St. Louis was 3,000 miles from Chihuahua, but a route from Austin to Chihuahua, by way of Santa Fé, would be only 2,000 miles; the savings and profits would be enormous if some or all of the trade could be diverted, and the Republic's economy was in dire need of such a stimulus. The Santa Fé traffic might constitute only part of a trading system which would include Cuba, should Spain approve. The Republic would trade horses, cattle and cotton for Cuban coffee, sugar, cigars and fruit which Texans were then purchasing in the United States. Substantial savings would accrue from a direct Cuban trade. The goods shipped from northern Mexico through Santa Fé to St. Louis would instead be hauled from Santa Fé to Austin and then to ports on the Gulf. The commercial activity would bind the Santa Fé area to the other settled parts of Texas despite hundreds of miles of Indian country separating them.

The Santa Fé Pioneers, as they were styled, began gathering near Austin in May, 1841. Numbering about 270 of the 320 participants, the military escort consisted of four mounted infantry companies and one artillery company. A few of the Pioneers were boys as young as twelve. Of the two dozen wagons, fourteen belonged to the merchants.

The Pioneers believed the people of Santa Fé would welcome them. George Wilkins Kendall, the New Orleans *Picayune* editor who accompanied the party wrote:

> On its arrival at the destined point, should the inhabitants really manifest a disposition to declare their full allegiance to Texas, the flag of the single-star Republic would have been raised on the Government House at Santa Fe; but if

President Mirabeau B. Lamar sponsored the Santa Fe Expedition to open trade with eastern New Mexico and bind that area to the rest of the Texas Republic.

not, the Texan Commissioners were merely to make such arrangements with the authorities as would best tend to the opening of a trade, and then retire.

He ridiculed allegations that the Pioneers were invaders bent on conquest; even with their mounted six-pound cannon, they could not have hoped to subdue a country of 150,000 people had all 320 men been trained soldiers unencumbered by merchandise. Kendall pointed out that by the time the expedition reached New Mexico it had failed and broken up; only weary and famished survivors of an ill-planned venture entered New Mexico. That they were armed proved nothing, for, "It cannot be considered very strange, then, that in a country so infested with hostile savages as Texas is, where a man hardly dares go out to catch his horse without a rifle and a pair of pistols about him, a military force accompanied this expedition." Enemies of the undertaking, Kendall charged, ". . . would have had us, forsooth, start off with walking sticks and umbrellas, and been scalped to a man in order to prove our object pacific." Having broken his ankle in Austin, Kendall traveled in a mule-drawn covered wagon with the lame José Navarro.

On the 18th of June, 1841, Lamar rode the fifteen miles to Camp Cazneau, the rendezvous on Brushy Creek in present Williamson County, to address the Pioneers on the importance of the expedition. Lamar cooked for himself and took care of his own horse.

The Pioneers departed on June 19 or 20 without adequate guides, for the western part of Texas was known only to the Indians. "Austin was in such a latitude and longitude and Santa Fé in another—of the principal part of the country between the two points not a man among us knew anything," stated Kendall. Captain Mathew Caldwell, a respected Indian fighter called "Old Paint" because of the heavy streaks of grey in his dark hair, tried to substitute for his lack of knowledge of the terrain his many years on the frontier. Caldwell's spy company was to remain a day's travel ahead of the main party in order to locate water, determine the best route, and watch for hostile Indians.

Early in the march a herd of mustangs startled the Pioneers, who thought they had come upon an Indian war party. Kendall admired the animals, which were in fine condition; smaller than American horses, they would "bear much fatigue." Kendall was intrigued by tales of the "White Steed of the Prairies." Substantial rewards had been offered for the stallion that outran race horses. Able to cover a mile in less than two minutes and maintain his pace long enough to shed all pursuers, he was always alone. According to an old hunter those solitary ways were due to his pride, "being an animal far superior in form and action to any of his brothers." Kendall wrote:

> Since my return I have been informed by a Texas gentleman, that a horse in many respects answering the description of the "White Steed of the Prairies" has been caught, after a hard chase, between the head waters of the Trinity and the Brazos. He lived but a short time, however, the excessive fatigue of the race causing his death.

A Pioneer committed suicide on June 25 and McLeod, because of illness, yielded command of the escort to Major Howard. By then it was clear that they should have departed in the early spring to be sure of good water and grazing for the animals. Discipline was poor. Because each man was to receive three pounds of beef daily, cattle were slaughtered at the same time men were shooting buffalo for recreation.

From Williamson County the expedition passed through the open, uninhabited country that is now Bell, McLennan and Bosque counties. The plan was to strike Red River and follow it west, probably because in the preceding year William Cooke and William Hunt had marked a route north to Red River. McLeod caught up with the party on July 12 and resumed command of the escort. The Pioneers cut across the corner of Hill County, passed through

Hugh McLeod commanded the military escort for the Santa Fe commissioners. He was captured, marched to Mexico, and imprisoned at Perote. He died in Virginia during the Civil War while commanding the First Texas Infantry and was buried in the State Cemetery in Austin.

Johnson County, and headed into the Cross Timbers in Parker County about July 21.

Morale, already in decline, was further impaired by the necessity of chopping down trees to get through the Cross Timbers. For a week, two dozen men spent all their time cutting a path. McLeod was having a hard time maintaining his position. To lighten loads he ordered tent poles and "all useless baggage" discarded. A quantity of dried beef was thrown away also.

The Pioneers emerged from the Cross Timbers in Montague County. On July 31, in Clay County, they encountered Indians for the first time. At an Indian village they concluded that they had found Red River; in fact, they were on the Wichita. They passed through present Wichita, Baylor, Knox, King, Cottle and Motley counties. One Carlos, claiming knowledge of the area, declared that they were near Santa Fé. On August 11 Samuel Howland and two others were sent ahead to get help. Realizing they were lost, Caldwell went north from Knox County in search of Red River. Carlos deserted. Many of the Pioneers were sick because of bad water. Kendall said, "We pushed on without rudder or compass, the melancholy truth visible in almost every face that we were lost among the wilderness prairies of the west."

In King County Indians stole half a dozen horses while the Pioneers slept and on August 30 Lieutenant Hull and a four-man scouting party were killed, "scalped, stripped and mutilated" by Kiowa. William Mabee's heart was cut out and there were more than two dozen wounds in Hull's body. (Expedition historian Thomas Falconer, an English barrister, said that the lieutenant's father was British Major General Trevor Hull.)

The desperately hungry Pioneers were eating prairie dogs and horses by August 31 when, just below the Caprock in western Motley County, the party divided. Cooke and a hundred of the strongest men set out to bring supplies from Santa Fé for the others, who waited with McLeod at "Camp Resolution" in present Floyd County. Cooke's party passed through Briscoe, Swisher and Deaf Smith counties, across the Staked Plains, and descended from the Caprock in New Mexico on September 7. There was no game, but Kendall wrote:

> . . . every tortoise and snake, every living and creeping thing was seized upon and swallowed by our famishing men with a rapacity that nothing but the direst hunger could induce. Occasionally a skunk or polecat would reward some more fortunate than the rest; but seven out of ten of us were compelled to journey on without a morsel of anything.

Finally they encountered New Mexicans who directed them to a settlement and were hired to bring the main party from Camp Resolution. Shepherds on the Rio Gallinas sold some sheep to Cooke's men, and "a scene of feasting ensued which beggars description." The shepherds reported that Mexican troops had arrested Howland, Baker and Rosenberry. On September 17, at San Miguel, according to Falconer:

> Howland and Baker were then taken to the upper end of the square, and bandages were put over their eyes. They were compelled to kneel down, and were shot in the back . . . . Rosenberry ineffectually resisted, and was killed when his friends were taken.

The unburied bodies were molested by dogs, then dragged to the edge of town and left to coyotes.

On that same day Cooke's party was captured at Anton Chico. The men were searched, robbed, and tied together. In the meantime McLeod remained at Camp Resolution where Indians took 83 horses and killed some men. In obedience to a message from Cooke, McLeod took his party onto the Caprock. On October 5 they surrendered to Governor Armijo on the promise of good treatment; they were plundered, bound and marched to San Miguel.

In this venture, which had been compared to the Lewis and Clark Expedition, another Lewis was involved. William P. Lewis was captured and then persuaded Cooke to surrender.

In appreciation General Armijo freed Lewis and gave him a share of the Pioneers' property. On his oath as a fellow Mason, Lewis had told Cooke that the Pioneers would be permitted to trade and would be given back their weapons and horses when they set out for home.

After Cooke's men marched thirty miles across rough country, Governor Armijo ordered them to return, without rest or food, to San Miguel. Armijo announced "They are able to walk ten leagues more. The Texans are an active and untiring people—I know them . . . if one of them *pretends* to be sick or tired on the road, *shoot him down and bring me his ears.*"

McLeod's party and the Cooke group were reunited at San Miguel on October 17 and they began the 2,000-mile walk to Mexico City. Many were barefoot. They were forced into a gait that daily yielded thirty to forty miles on feet which were frostbitten at night, when it usually snowed. Armijo had taken their coats and second blankets.

Falconer wrote of one Ernest, who died of exhaustion:

> He had suffered much from the long marches of the previous days. His ears were cut off to be presented by our captain to his superior officer as evidence that the man had not escaped, and this barbarous proceeding occurred in every instance, on the road, either of natural death, or of murder.

When John McAllister complained that he could not move faster because of his sore feet, "He was almost instantly shot through the head. His ears were cut off, his blanket and pantaloons taken from him and his body left on the road."

Through the Jornada del Muerto (the Journey of the Dead), a 90-mile stretch above Juarez, the men were permitted no rest. There was no water, it was bitterly cold, and the Mexicans killed more prisoners. At Paso del Norte the officer in charge, Salazar, handed his superior five pairs of ears strung on a strip of buckskin.

Reaching Mexico City about February 1, 1842, the survivors were imprisoned at Santiago, Perote and Puebla. Some were released that April and May. Except for Navarro, who was confined in Mexico's worst prison, the Acordada, the rest were freed on June 13, 1842, President Antonio Lopez de Santa Anna's fiftieth birthday. (Navarro escaped in January of 1845.)

Colonel Hugh McLeod, commander of the 1st Texas Regiment, died during the Civil War at Dumfries, Virginia. Dr. Richard Brenham and about twenty others were members of the Mier expedition and were again captives of the Mexicans. Brenham was killed in an escape attempt. Falconer spent the last thirty years of his life as a judge in Wales.

In analyzing the expedition's failure Kendall mentioned the late start and consequent scarcity of water and grass, the lack of qualified guides which cost the Pioneers 300 miles, and delays resulting from the Republic's failure to furnish sufficient wagons. More cattle should have been provided and they should not have been slaughtered while buffalo were available. The Indian problem had been worse than anticipated. Finally, Lamar had misjudged the character of Armijo, although his assessment of the attitudes of the Santa Fé populace had been accurate. Kendall stated:

> Not a doubt can exist that they all were, and are, anxious to throw off the oppressive yoke of Armijo and come under the liberal institutions of Texas; but the governor found us divided into small parties; broken down by long marches and want of food; discovered, too, a traitor among us; and, taking advantage of these circumstances, his course was plain, and his conquest easy.

Somervell Went in Pursuit of the Mexican Invaders

When Sam Houston again became president on December 13, 1841, the financial condition of the Republic of Texas was critical. He told the Congress:

> There is not a dollar in the treasury. The nation is involved from ten to fifteen millions. The precise amount of its liability has not been ascertained . . . . We are not only without money, but without credit, and, for want of punctuality, without character.

Word reached Texas on January 18, 1842, that members of the Santa Fé expedition had been imprisoned in Mexico. The angry Congress then passed an act extending the boundaries of the Republic to take in two-thirds of Mexico. Houston vetoed the bill and otherwise restrained the legislators, for the Republic was too broke to strike at Mexico and talk of hostilities would retard the flow of immigrants to Texas. Houston declared, "Peace will bring with it every advantage."

Ever since the battle of San Jacinto invasion had been threatened by Mexican officials who refused to acknowledge that Texas was independent but knew Mexico was not strong enough for reconquest. As the annexation of Texas to the United States was sought, proponents argued that Mexico's failure for six years to mount an invasion was equivalent to recognition of the independence of Texas. On March 5, 1842, acting pursuant to orders of President Santa Anna, an army under General Rafael Vasquez captured San Antonio, raised the flag of Mexico, appointed an alcalde, and declared Mexican laws to be in force; two days later Vasquez withdrew. His 700 soldiers took everything they considered to be of value. Two other small Mexican forces occupied Refugio and Goliad for awhile. Samuel Walker estimated that Vasquez's army took property worth $30,000.

Jack Hays and about a hundred men followed the Mexicans to the Nueces, but no battle occurred. General Edward Burleson arrived in San Antonio with about 300 volunteers on March 15. Knowing the Republic could not afford to act, with reluctance Houston called up the militia. Brigadier General Alexander Somervell was to form the men into an army, but the volunteers at San Antonio, numbering more than 3,000, were committed to Vice President Burleson. Before an invasion could be launched money would have to be borrowed from friends in the United States. The volunteers wanted prompt action, for they could not afford to be away from their farms for very long.

Ignoring his commitment to independence made in the Treaties of Velasco, Santa Anna now threatened conquest. Yoakum quoted Houston's advice to the Congress:

> No formidable invasion, it is true, has been attempted since 1836, nor do I believe they will ever be able to effect its accomplishment; but, though this is my firm conviction, I am nevertheless equally satisfied that they will interpose every impediment to the peace, prosperity, and settlement of our frontier.

On September 22, 1842, General Adrian Woll, a French soldier of fortune, led an army of 1,200 into San Antonio. After killing twelve and wounding 29 of the invaders and suffering no casualties, the handful of defenders surrendered as prisoners of war. Woll left Bexar on the

Captain Samuel Walker, one of the great Texas Ranger captains, suggested changes in the Colt revolver and a grateful Samuel Colt called his improved model the Walker Colt. Walker accompanied Somervell to the border and was captured with the Mier Expedition and imprisoned in Mexico. He was killed in the Mexican War.

20th, taking with him 53 prisoners, including Judge Hutchinson and the lawyers, parties, witnesses and everyone else present at the District Court. Woll also carried into captivity the fifteen survivors of the Dawson massacre, in which 36 Texans were killed.

Texans demanded retaliation. Although the bankrupt Republic was in no condition for war the Mexican invasions could not be ignored. Thomas Bell recalled that "by voluntary subscription arms, ammunition and supplies were being raised for those willing to engage in the service, and General Houston finding popular sentiment too strongly in favor of the expedition to be withstood, ordered out the militia under Brigadier General Somervell . . . ." Somervell was to

> . . . proceed to the most eligible point on the southwestern frontier of Texas . . . and if you can advance with a prospect of success into the enemy's territory, you will do so forthwith . . . . You will . . . receive no troops into your command, but such as will march across the Rio Grande under your orders if required to do so.

Somervell reached San Antonio on November 4. Morale was poor, for the volunteers had been waiting for several days and they preferred the popular Burleson to Somervell. The weather was bad and supplies were hard to come by. The Army assembled at Camp Cooke on the Medina twenty miles from San Antonio and on November 25, 1842, Somervell led about 750 volunteers and militia toward Mexico, seeking to avenge the plundering of San Antonio, Refugio and Goliad and hoping to obtain hostages to trade for Woll's captives.

Winter was coming on. Thomas Jefferson Green wrote that the men acquired warmer clothing

> by transferring the covering of many an unwary buck to their own legs. I never saw deer so plentiful; many hundreds were killed, and the whole camp for several days had more the appearance of a tremendous tanyard than an army which expected in a few days to meet the national enemy upon his own soil.

In Green's opinion the troops "had the smallest confidence" in Somervell's leadership but were so eager for battle they would have followed "a crooked stick." Instead of the anticipated seven days the march to Laredo required seventeen. The rain turned the ground into such a bog that finding sufficient firm land to make camp was difficult.

On the evening of December 7 the Texans arrived at the Rio Grande. They prepared to attack Laredo, for although it was a Texas town officials held their appointments through the government of Mexico and the general assumed that Mexican troops might be waiting there. Samuel Walker wrote:

> At daylight we surrounded the town & took town & the alcalde was informed of our mission and we received possession of it without resistance. We marched & encamped about 1 league from town. The men were hungry & no grass for their horses and no assurance that their wants should be supplied by a requisition. No guard was placed to prevent the men from going to town. The consequence was that many of the men were in the town and some of them commenced plundering by taking such things as was necessary to their actual wants.

Outraged by looting which occurred in violation of Somervell's order to respect private property, Bell stated:

> Many things were carried into camp by the robbers, which were immediately taken from them and returned to the owners that evening. This town situated as it is in Texas and its inhabitants not making even a show of resistance to the entrance of the Texans, it was nothing less than downright robbery to make booty of their property. This disgraceful transaction was therefore severely

censured by a large majority of the army, both officers and privates, and the offenders justly held up to public contempt and ridicule.

Somervell's apology began, "I regret to learn that some bad men belonging to the army under my command committed acts of outrage in your town." Emphasizing that most of his men disapproved of the plundering, he promised reparations. Blaming Somervell for failing to provide supplies he had promised, Green contended that the rules of war "gave these men a perfect right to take all necessaries for their subsistence" and faulted the general for not defining the items they might legitimately seize.

Morale worsened as the army marched down the Rio Grande without invading Mexico. Christmas was coming. The men needed to be with their families, especially if there was to be no fighting. Many, including the conscripted militiamen, decided to go home, for their mission was accomplished in that Texas was free of Mexican troops. In support of their decision, some gave as their reason an unwillingness to serve longer with the despoilers of Laredo. About 200 departed and the others descended the river and levied upon the Mexican town of Guerrero a requisition which yielded meager supplies.

When on December 19 Somervell ordered a return march to the confluence of the Nueces and Frio and then to Gonzales, where the army would disband, only 189 of the 500 men obeyed, among them Colonel William G. Cooke who, recently released from prison in Mexico, had married Angela Navarro, the niece of his fellow Santa Fé commissioner, José Antonio Navarro; Colonel John Hemphill, who would later be United States Senator from Texas; Captain Peter Bell, who would become governor; and John C. Hays. Although some of those who ignored the order were motivated by a desire for action, probably most simply believed they were unprepared for the journey. Bell wrote:

> But being destitute of the supplies requisite to accomplish a march of nearly three hundred miles, at this inclement season of the year and that mostly through an uninhabited country where nothing could be obtained for sustenance but game; therefore three hundred volunteers under the command of Col. W. S. Fisher, not by any means satisfied with what had been thus far effected, (which was nothing more than striking a panic into this part of the territory) and having entered the army and marched here with the expectation of meeting the enemy in battle, and having been thus far disappointed, it was thought not at all improper to remain awhile longer, and at some favorable opportunity give the tawny sons of Montezuma undeniable proof of what they might expect to receive at the hands of Texas . . . .

These dissenters elected William S. Fisher to lead them. The second in command, Green, remarked, "The general started home with two hundred and odd men; including his extensive staff, numerous enough for a field-marshal of France, while he left behind him three hundred and four men to do the fighting." Bell believed Somervell should have

> made a bold and vigorous push across the Rio Grande when he first struck it and marched down its western bank, instead of lingering on his own dunghill and allowing the timid part of his army to conjure up imaginary enemies; the towns of Mier, Camargo, Reynoso and even the city of Matamoras itself, might easily have been invested with far less destruction of human life than afterward occurred . . . .

Writing soon after returning from Mexico, Bell doubtless was recalling his 21 months in prison and numerous attendant horrors, including participation in the drawing of the black beans at Salado Ranch.

Somervell's party broke up on the return march. After great suffering because of lack of food and winter clothing, the last of those who left the Rio Grande with Somervell arrived in San Antonio on January 8, 1843.

The Mier Prisoners Were Marched to Mexico City

After the invasion of Texas by Mexican armies and the kidnapping of everyone attending the San Antonio district court, General Alexander Somervell led an army of militiamen and volunteers to the Rio Grande. When, on December 19, 1842, Somervell ordered the return march, 304 men refused to obey; in this fashion the Mier expedition was formed.

Colonel William S. Fisher was elected to lead the dissenters. His command was divided into six companies, the largest led by Ewen Cameron. Fisher marched the main body down the north bank while Thomas Jefferson Green, second in command, set out by water with four flatboats and four canoes manned by sixty men. Green was surprised by the size of the Rio Grande:

> ... we descended it at a low stage of water—on few occasions does it get lower—and never found any place at which it could be forded below Laredo, and it is, indeed, barely fordable there. It is a beautiful river, averaging four hundred yards in width, with high bluffs generally on one side or the other . . . .

By December 22 the infantry and "navy" had come together about seven miles from Mier, a town of 7,000 which, except for Matamoras, was the wealthiest on the Rio Grande. Scouts reported General Pedro Ampudia en route with a large army; nevertheless, on the following morning Fisher invaded Mier. Claiming his force numbered 1,200 he demanded all of the town's weapons and ammunition, 40 sacks of flour, 1,200 pounds of sugar, 600 pounds of coffee, 200 pairs of shoes, 100 blankets and 100 pairs of trousers. The Texans crossed the river to await delivery of the supplies, holding the alcalde hostage. (To prevent escape Mier's poor alcalde was forced to sleep with one leg between the legs of Green, whom he called Commodore Verde.)

Bell thought Fisher would order a return to San Antonio after the requisition was filled, "judging very reasonably that with his small force it would be useless and even hazardous to remain longer on the border of the enemy's country, and thereby give them time to bring a force of far superior number to bear upon his inconsiderable numbers."

Soon after Fisher made his requisition, General Ampudia arrived with nearly three thousand troops and the next day he tried to catch the Texans; he waited

> where the authorities of the town were to deliver the supplies, intending, instead of delivering supplies of flour and beef to the Texan Colonel and his ragmuffin followers, to issue to them a few thousand blue pills hurled by fire and brimstone from a convenient distance across the Rio Grande river, to cure them of a disease with which he supposed they must be extremely afflicted, viz that of marching three hundred miles to kill and rob the Mexicans.

Having missed the rendezvous Fisher was unaware of Ampudia's presence until on Christmas Day a captured soldier reported that the Mexican general had kept the merchants from filling the requisition. To Bell's amazement Fisher ordered an attack.

> A large trail had been discovered and reported by the scouts, afterwards ascertained to have been made by the Mexican army going to and from the river

The main street of Mier, Mexico, across from Roma, where the men of the Mier Expedition, under the command of Colonel William Fisher, fought a bloody engagement and then surrendered.

the previous evening. Two scouts had been captured or killed the day before, and three others narrowly escaped by running. With all these facts so glaringly staring them in the face it can hardly be credited that a set of men would thus blindly rush to their own destruction; yet they did it and led others who unwittingly confiding in the judgment of their officers followed without flinching.

Leaving horses and baggage in charge of 43 sick and injured men, Fisher crossed the river. Bell wrote:

> Just as the joyous laugh of the giddy and the gay was merrily ringing throughout all Christendom, rejoicing in the festivity of the day, or the pious prayers of the humble and devout Christian were ascending to the throne of the Most High for the reign of peace and good will among the sons of fallen man; at this time two races destined never to be friends were preparing to imbrue their hands in each others blood . . . .

The Texans fought their way into Mier. After dark they moved into two stone houses a hundred yards from the north side of the square. After inflicting heavy losses, the Texans discovered in the morning light "the housetops and streets lined with Mexican soldiers." About noon a Mexican soldier came forward under a flag of truce. The Texans thought Ampudia wished to capitulate; instead their own surrender was demanded.

Of 261 Texans in the battle ten were killed and six of the two dozen wounded died later. Stapp wrote:

> The Mexican force opposed to us exceeded thirty-two hundred, of which about four hundred were cavalry, and the balance infantry. Of these, upwards of six hundred were slain, and the number of wounded never ascertained. The faces of many of the houses on whose terraces the enemy were posted, were flecked with blood, and numerous sanguinary stains discoloured the pavements beneath.

Later the Texans learned that Ampudia had planned to retreat had they refused to surrender. Most of his men preferred to fight, but Fisher argued that Ampudia was an honorable man and submission the only rational course. Half the men marched out to the square to surrender. Green recalled:

> Now a scene commenced which defies description. In the countenances of those whom Colonel Fisher's speech did not induce to surrender, were disappointment, sorrow, rage: many shed tears, some swore, while others maintained a sullen determination, which showed that they were prepared for the worst.

They shouted insults and warnings as they watched their comrades "marched into captivity in silent obedience." Then Green and the rest surrendered.

That evening the prisoners' supper was an insufficient quantity of boiled beef served in a kettle, with no plates, cups, or knives. On the first day they marched 25 miles without water and after a meal of half-boiled beef, Bell wrote, they:

> lay down on the ground for a bed and the sky for a covering, during a cold frosty night in the month of December; therefore shivering with cold and hovering over a few little brushwood fires, they spent the night cursing their hard fate; but they little dreamed that this was only the beginning and a mere introduction to what was yet to come.

A few days later a runaway Texas slave called to Green, "Aha! white man, dey cotch you now; dey gib you hell!" William P. Stapp observed:

> For the first time the revolting consciousness came over us, we were prisoners, and in the power of Santa Anna, the unscrupulous butcher of Goliad and Bexar. The green graves of six hundred of his soldiers appealed against us for vengeance on their slayers; and who that ever heard of his reckless contempt of

John Reagan Baker was sheriff of Refugio County before joining the Somervell and Mier Expeditions. Wounded in the break at Rancho Salado, he was walked to Mexico City and imprisoned at Perote. Born in 1809, Baker died on his Wilson County ranch in 1904.

faith with friend and foe, but felt how vain was the hope to escape his retribution.

The prisoners were put on display in the river towns. For a week they remained at Matamoras, where a German merchant, J. P. Schatzell, provided for their immediate needs and gave them spending money totaling about $3,000. On meager rations they walked about 25 miles a day. They reached Saltillo on February 5, 1843, and six days later, at Rancho Salado, Captain Ewen Cameron led an escape. Richard Brenham, killed in the break, had only recently been a Santa Fé Pioneer imprisoned in Mexico. Approximately twenty who did not join the attempt remained with the sick and wounded. There had been better chances for success earlier, but as the guards' behavior presaged harsher treatment—Colonel Barragan having approved the flogging of prisoners—most of the Texans joined Cameron.

Had the escapees remained on the main road they would have reached the border safely, but becoming frightened they scattered into the mountains where, after six days without water, they threw away their arms and were recaptured. Bell stated:

> The picture of misery that presented itself as this suffering group of men were marshalled into the Mexican camp was truly of a distressing character and baffles the power of language to describe it. Their eyes were sunken far back in the sockets and seemed to have lost the lustre of human intelligences. Their death-like visages covered with dust, gave them the appearance of a congregation of the dead more than living mortals, and their feeble voices as they cried for water and begged with tears their inhuman captors, only to give them a little of that cooling fluid.

The fugitives were tied in couples with rawhide thongs, which later were replaced by heavy iron handcuffs, "and with these they afterward marched several hundred miles in the most excruciating pain." At Santiago they were fitted with ankle chains weighing about ten pounds apiece and were thus fettered until they reached Mexico City in September of 1843. At Saltillo General Francisco Mexía's refusal to carry out Santa Anna's execution order against all of the captives resulted in the loss of his command. The 176 prisoners were marched back to Rancho Salado and Santa Anna ordered every tenth man shot. Stapp wrote:

> Who can describe the thrill of horror . . . when the interpreter, in broken and tremulous tones, announced it as an order from the supreme government, directing every tenth man amongst us to be shot! the lots to be decided on the instant, and the execution to follow immediately. So entirely unexpected was this murderous announcement, so atrocious in its character, and so inhuman and indecent in the haste of its consummation, that a stupor seemed to pervade the whole assembly, not a word escaping from the lips of any for more than a minute.

On March 25, at Rancho Salado, the Mexicans placed in a crock one bean for each escapee, 159 white and 17 black, and each man was required to draw forth a bean in the manner described by Stapp:

> A handkerchief, so folded as to hide the colour of the beans, was then thrown over the crock, and a list of our names, taken down when we were recaptured, placed in the hands of the interpreter . . . . Each name continued to be called in their order on the list, and the individual compelled to draw, until the seventeen black beans were taken from the crock. When a bean was drawn, it was handed to the officer, and the bowl well shaken before the lottery proceeded. As they drew, each person's name was entered upon another memorandum, with the colour of his bean. In many instances the doomed victim was enforced to revisit the fatal urn, to allow the comrade to whom he was chained to try the issues of life and death.

48

William Stapp, one of the Mier prisoners, wrote a book about his captivity in Mexico.

W. A. A. (Bigfoot) Wallace realized the black beans were larger than the white ones and saved himself by being able to distinguish between them. After digging their own graves the Texans were shot by a firing squad. Sixteen died immediately; James L. Shepherd was only wounded and escaped. Weeks later he was caught, taken to Saltillo, where he was recognized and, Stapp says, was "led directly to the public square and shot to death, amidst the pitiless exultations of its citizens."

On the night of April 24 at an hacienda near Mexico City the prisoners were confined in such small rooms they could not lie down "and into which not a breath of air could enter when the door was closed." Green, who with the other officers were kept apart from the men, stated:

> They in vain appealed to the guards at the door to let in fresh air, and when death the most cruel stared them wholesale in the face, as a last alternative they had recourse to cutting holes in the door with their pocket knives, and alternately breathing at these small orifices.
> This was, indeed, as the Mexican soldiers called it, la noche triste, "the sad night." Their march of many leagues the day before, through an insufferable dust, a burning sun, the want of food and water, and then at night not even space sufficient on the stone floor to lie upon, and a suffocating atmosphere to breathe, was not their full measure of woe. About eight o'clock at night a menial murderer . . . arrived with orders from the tyrant Santa Anna to shoot the bold and beloved Captain Ewen Cameron. The ill-starred Cameron, who had already shared the risks of the cruel and perilous lottery at the Salado, was awakened . . . and being hurried half naked into a distant room, was unceremoniously informed he was to be shot next morning . . . .

Mexican officials explained that Cameron's life was required because only 17 had been shot; since every tenth man of the 176 escapees was condemned, a fraction, 6/10 of a man, remained and had to be made up.

A few days earlier some prisoners had bought vino mescal and ingredients for egg nog to celebrate the seventh anniversary of the San Jacinto victory. Green remembered:

> When those noble fellows stood round the bowl in rags, with their "jewelry" riveted upon their ankles . . . the sight filled my heart to overflowing. Though the body was oppressed, they looked like caged lions, and every face bespoke the invincible spirit of a freeman.

In September, 1843, 126 of the Texans were lodged in the prison of Perote in the state of Vera Cruz. Twenty-two of the prisoners died there. Green was one of those who effected an escape. From time to time the Mier men were released, but most were set free in September of 1844. Stapp had been freed in the preceding May by virtue of the efforts of relatives in the United States. Bell delivered a message from the dying O. R. Willis to his wife in Tennessee and married the widow Willis; they raised a large family, and after Bell's death she moved to Texas. Recalling the horrors of Santa Anna's lottery, Bell stated: "The kindest treatment these captives ever received from any Mexican never could erase from their memories the bloody tragedy of the Salado."

This group of Mier prisoners was photographed soon after being freed from their year and a half in Mexican prisons. Third from left is Henry Journeay.

Using only a razor and a piece of glass, Henry Journeay made this fiddle while he was imprisoned at Perote.

John Rufus Alexander, one of the Mier prisoners, took part in the break at Rancho Salado and was among the four who were not recaptured. This photograph was taken during the 1870's.

Navarro Was The Stern and Honest Patriot

Angel Navarro was born in 1739 at Ajaccio, Corsica, thirty years before Napoleon Bonaparte's birth there. Navarro sailed to Mexico as a seventeen-year-old private in Spain's army. While stationed in Saltillo, Navarro married Josepha Ruíz, a native of San Antonio. In 1777 Navarro, by then a colonel, was assigned to Indian service in Texas.

After leaving the army Navarro opened a store in San Antonio on the northeast corner of Flores and Commerce streets, across from Main Plaza, and in 1790 he became the alcalde. The Navarros' twelve children, all born in San Antonio, were seven boys named José and five girls named María. Angel Navarro died in 1808 and was buried in the cemetery that is now Milam Square.

José Antonio Navarro, the Corsican's eighth child, was born February 27, 1795. He was fifteen when Father Miguel Hidalgo began Mexico's revolution and San Antonio's population of about 3,000 was augmented by 2,000 troops sent to hold Texas against the rebels. Many of those soldiers helped local rebels arrest the governor and other officials in 1811. That revolution was overthrown and in the ensuing turmoil General Joaquin Arredondo almost depopulated San Antonio; Navarro, his brothers, and their uncle, Francisco Ruíz, fled to the United States.

Navarro had little formal education but he studied law and became an attorney. He was also a merchant and rancher. In 1825 he married Margarita de la Garza, of Mier. A Catholic, a Mason, and a member of the legislature of Coahuila y Texas, Navarro assisted Stephen F. Austin's colonization efforts by helping pass laws protecting colonists' interests in slaves and prohibiting the forced sale of land in debt actions, foreshadowing the homestead provisions of the Texas constitution. Navarro was the land commissioner for De Witt's colony and later for Bexar. After serving in the Mexican Congress, in 1835 Navarro was elected to the Senate but did not take his seat.

At Washington-on-the-Brazos, on March 2, 1836, Navarro and his uncle, Francisco Ruíz, signed the declaration of independence. Navarro helped write the constitution of the Republic. His store was looted and most of his cattle stolen during the seige of the Alamo. (The son of Ruíz was San Antonio's alcalde and Jim Bowie, who died at the Alamo, was the husband of Navarro's niece, Ursula Veramendi. Navarro's brother, José Angel, the political chief of Bexar, remained loyal to Mexico.)

One of Jack Hays' Rangers, James Nichols, wrote of Navarro's character:

> At the time I speak of he had near two hundred acres in a farm (near Seguin) and kept from 12 to 15 peons or slave families on his ranch besides from 20 to 30 single men, all Mexicans. He had near three thousand head of cattle and five or six hundred head of horses . . . . He went (on) the Santafe expedition. They were all taken prisoners and marched to Mexico . . . the authorities offered him his liberty if he would cut the Lone Star button off his coat. He said he would die in prison before he would disgrace the caus of Texas.

A member of the Third and Fourth Congresses of the Republic of Texas, Navarro was a civil commissioner of the Santa Fé expedition responsible for taking charge of the local

José Navarro was one of the two native Texans who signed the Declaration of Texas Independence. He was confined in the worst of the Mexican prisons after being captured with other members of the Santa Fe Expedition.

government if that could be done peacefully. The people of Santa Fé were to be reminded of their Texas citizenship and trade relations were to be established. General Manuel Armijo captured the entire company. Navarro was given especially severe treatment for his part in the Texas revolution. An accident in youth had left Navarro lame. He had been riding in a wagon but the Mexicans made him walk. The early part of the forced march to Mexico so badly damaged his injured leg that he could neither sit in a saddle nor could he stand. A Chihuahua citizen, appalled by the captives' plight, gave them clothing and provided Navarro a mule and cart.

Dr. Joseph Dawson's fine biography contains a letter from Navarro saying, "If you do not intercede, I shall die, possibly on this road, almost certainly when we arrive in the Capital." The prisoners trudged through the rough country, Dawson said, "with no joyous prospects of anything good awaiting one or all at journey's end, a trek unparalleled in Western history, the mildest account of which upsets the nerves of the hardened even after more than a hundred years have passed."

The other prisoners were released after several months in Mexican prisons but not Navarro. George Wilkins Kendall wrote of Santa Anna's special persecution of Navarro:

> Not content with simply depriving him of liberty the heartless tyrant kept him constantly confined in the vilest and most filthy prisons, and among the lowest malefactors. Over and over again was he offered liberty, station and wealth, if he would turn against Texas, or use his influence to bring her back into the Mexican confederacy; but inflexibly pure, the stern and honest patriot spurned every effort with disdain.

Navarro was condemned to die, but his execution was set aside on appeal because when they surrendered Armijo promised the Pioneers their lives. Infuriated by the reversal but unable to change it, Santa Anna commuted Navarro's sentence to life on September 24, 1842. Kendall stated:

> Enraged at being thus foiled, Santa Anna sent his incorruptible prisoner to that worst of all places in Mexico, the castle of San Juan de Ulloa at Vera Cruz, with orders that he should be confined, solitary and alone, in the darkest, dampest, dreariest dungeon within its walls. He must have thought and hoped that death would at least soon reach him in that unhealthy hole, and there would be an end of one he did not dare openly order to execution.
>
> The month of December, 1844, found Mr. Navarro still incarcerated in his loathsome dungeon, deprived of light, of all communication with friends, of everything save his own high sense of patriotism, of honor and love of country. But a day of reckoning was soon to fall upon his industrious persecutor, for in the same month Santa Anna was forcibly driven from place and power by the fickle population of Mexico, deprived of all his rights, and booted with ignominy out of the country after humbly supplicating for his miserable life.

Navarro had been chained to the floor of his cell. After Santa Anna's fall he was permitted to move about the prison, which was on an island. As he was out walking one day an American in a passing boat invited him aboard; Navarro's escape was as simple as that. Santa Anna's successor as president, General Herrera, made no attempt to recapture him. Taken to Havana, then to New Orleans, Navarro landed in Galveston on February 15, 1845. After four years he returned home.

At the annexation convention, on July 4, 1845, Navarro voted for joinder to the United States and helped draw a state constitution. Although he was a fine Spanish orator, Navarro never mastered English. Reuben Potter and George Fisher were among those who interpreted for him. Navarro was a member of the first Senate of the State of Texas; when his

The home of José Antonio Navarro, on Laredo Street in San Antonio, is dwarfed by neighboring buildings.

colleagues named a new county for him, he suggested that Navarro County's seat be Corsicana in memory of his father, Angel Navarro, the Corsican.

Navarro took no part in the secession movement. He died January 14, 1871, of cancer of the tongue which he believed was caused by his constant smoking of homemade cigarettes. (The president at the time, U. S. Grant, later wrote of the habit as he had seen it during the war with Mexico:

> Almost every Mexican above the age of ten years, and many much younger, smoked the cigarette. Nearly every Mexican carried a pouch of leaf tobacco, powdered by rolling in the hands, and a roll of corn husks to make wrappers. The cigarettes were made by the smokers as they used them.)

Navarro's home, at Laredo and Nueva streets in San Antonio, has been restored and is operated by the Department of Parks and Wildlife.

Navarro's store and law office occupy part of his homesite.

José Antonio Navarro died in this room of cancer, which he said was caused by cigarettes.

Navarro County was created and named in his honor while José Antonio Navarro was a member of the State Senate. Navarro suggested the county seat be called Corsicana for his father, Angel Navarro, who was born on Corsica.

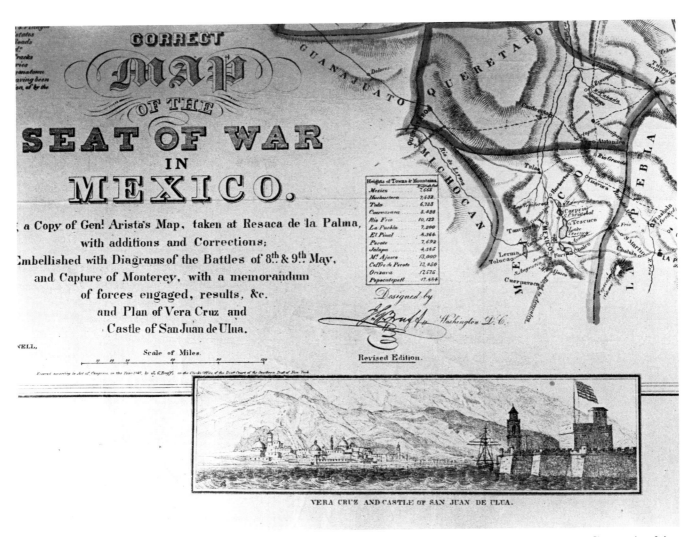

CORRECT **MAP** OF THE SEAT OF WAR IN **MEXICO.**

a Copy of Gen! Arista's Map, taken at Resaca de la Palma,
with additions and Corrections;
Embellished with Diagrams of the Battles of 8th & 9th May,
and Capture of Monterey, with a memorandum
of forces engaged, results, &c.
and Plan of Vera Cruz and
Castle of San Juan de Ulua.

Scale of Miles.

Heights of Towns & Mountains	
Mexico	7,668
Huehuetoca	7,632
Tula	6,735
Cuernavaca	5,438
Rio Frio	10,122
La Puebla	7,200
El Pinal	8,366
Perote	7,692
Jalapa	4,335
M! Ajusco	13,000
Coffre de Perote	13,450
Orizava	17,375
Popocatepetl	17,884

Designed by

Washington D.C.

Revised Edition.

VERA CRUZ AND CASTLE OF SAN JUAN DE ULUA.

–Texas State Archives

This map, published in 1847, has a drawing of the Ulloa prison at Vera Cruz where Navarro
was imprisoned after confinement in the Accordada—called by T. J. Green "the most loath-
some and infamous prison in Mexico, where he, for more than two years, suffered more than
the horrors of death." He escaped from the Castle of San Juan Ulloa, in the harbor where
Cortes began his conquest of Mexico in 1519.

Col. José Antonio Navarro
signer of the Declaration
of Texas Independence
and the hero of the
Santa Fe Expedition.

Navarro, a commissioner of the Santa Fe Expedition was captured in New Mexico and held in the worst prisons of Mexico, the Acordada and San Juan de Ulloa, by Santa Anna in an attempt to kill him.

Noah T. Byars Organized Baptist Churches

Noah Turner Byars, born in South Carolina on May 17, 1808, grew up on a farm and learned blacksmithing and gunsmithing. Despite a limited education he wanted to be a Baptist minister. After four years in Georgia, in April of 1835 he settled at Washington, the village at the Brazos River crossing of the Atascosito Road, which connected Nacogdoches, La Bahía and Laredo. Washington-on-the-Brazos had a population of about two dozen, half of them drifters whose main interests were gambling and horseracing.

Byars built a gun shop on the south side of Main Street. He offered the services of his apprentice and journeyman to settlers preparing to defend against their former hero, Santa Anna, who now promised to show them no mercy. In that it was the only structure of sufficient size, Byars rented his building to the convention which met in March of 1836 and declared Texas to be independent of Mexico. He was never paid the rent—three months at $56 per month—he had been promised. Dr. John Lockhart left this description of Byars' famous building:

> It was a one-story house with the gable toward the street, and situated immediately on the street with a double door in the center opening on the street with one or two steps leading to it . . . none of the windows had glass in them but were closed by wooden shutters . . . . The house was about 25 feet in width by about 50 feet in length, was an ordinary frame, weather boarded with common clap boards split with a fro and smoothed with a drawing knife.

The building had no ceiling. Later it was used as a store and public hall, and "one of the Greatest Christian Revivals" took place as the Reverend William Tryon and Judge R. E. B. Baylor, founders of Baylor University,

> held a protracted meeting there . . . . There were only two or three who did not join the church. It was a curious and solemn sight to see from ten to fifteen candidates for baptism arise from their seats and follow their pastors to the Brazos river at 9 or 10 o'clock at night to receive the ordinance of baptism; and the very water that was to cleanse them from their sins had perhaps only a few hours previously laved the bodies of beastly savages not far up the river.

Dr. T. R. Havins quoted a poem Byars had composed in the early days of the revolution, which advised:

> Boys, rub your steel and pick your flints,
> Methinks I hear some friendly hints,
> That we from Texas shall be driven
> Our lands to Spanish soldiers given,
> To arms, to arms, to arms!

For awhile Byars was armorer to Sam Houston's army. In applying for payment Byars wrote of himself:

> And in order to serve his country to the full extent of his ability he left his journeyman and one apprentice in the shop in Washington, he paying their board himself at the tavern, and instructing them to work on the arms of every person going to the field without charge while your petitioner repaired himself to the field and performed the services of armorer there until his health failed

–Brownwood Lodge No. 279, A. F. & A. M.

Noah T. Byars owned the building in which the Texas Declaration of Independence was signed. He was for many years a missionary Baptist preacher and founded churches in Waco, Brownwood, Corsicana, Belton and elsewhere.

him so much that he was compelled to return but still carried on his shop in Washington until he had repaired upward of 500 stands of arms.

Byars served as the Texas Senate sergeant-at-arms from 1836 to 1839. After marrying Mrs. Sophia Lowden, a widow, in 1838 he moved to Bastrop and became justice of the peace. Byars was a Travis County justice when he decided to become a minister. In October of 1841 he was ordained by the Macedonia Baptist Church, the Reverend Z. N. Morrell and the Reverend John Woodruff officiating before witnesses which included President M. B. Lamar and members of his cabinet.

In 1842 the Reverend Noah T. Byars settled on a 3,129-acre tract at Dresden. He built a log house and sold 435 acres to raise funds to buy cattle. At his first church, in Burleson County, he erected an impressive building. Since Byars received no salary he accepted whatever work was offered; in 1845 he served as blacksmith and armorer for some Indians under commission of the Republic. In the next three years, supporting himself mainly through notary public fees, Byars organized six churches in Navarro, Limestone and Leon counties, they created the Trinity River Baptist Association, Judge R. E. B. Baylor presiding, in 1848.

In 1846 Byars attended a meeting called by General Edward H. Tarrant to consider the necessity of carving a new county from the territory of Robertson County, and later that year Navarro County was created, with Corsicana the seat of government. (Byars officiated at the marriage of Tarrant and Miss Danforth at Dresden in April, 1851.)

The new Baptist State Convention hired Byars to do missionary work in Navarro County in 1849. Searching out Baptists and organizing churches, in three months Byars preached twenty sermons and traveled 500 miles, for which he was paid $25. Because of his successes, in June, 1850, $75 was appropriated to support Byars as a missionary at Waco, which was well into Indian country. On May 31, 1851, he organized the First Baptist Church "in a board shanty on the corner of Jackson and Second streets" in Waco. The congregation met in a structure of cedar poles with plank doors and window shutters. The 3½ years at that church was his longest pastorate, for Byars was mainly an organizer.

Representing the state organization, Byars moved to Birdville, Tarrant County, and was moderator for the new twelve-member West Fork Baptist Association. Then, living in Parker County, in three months of 1856 he covered 1,320 miles, gave 45 sermons and nine lectures, organized a church, and visited 127 families and the Brazos Indian Reservation. Byars sought schools for the 299 children under twelve at Fort Belknap and 250 at Camp Cooper. Both Captain Ross, the Fort Belknap agent, and Captain Baylor, the agent for the Comanche near Camp Cooper, favored the opening of Indian schools; Byars and Sam Houston urged unsuccessfully their establishment at the Baptists' annual convention in Huntsville.

In 1856 Byars organized four Palo Pinto County churches. Constantly working in the hinterland he complained, "My salary, at best, away in this frontier will not support me, and I am positively distressed. I do not have a child in school although all of them need to be." Through his efforts a school was built in Palo Pinto just prior to the Civil War.

As the years passed Byars did not slow his pace. In Brown County, where there were 500 residents, many living in tents, he, the Reverend J. M. Perry, and eight members organized, on February 19, 1876, the First Baptist Church, which met monthly for six years in the courthouse until the commissioners forbade further religious use of the premises and the congregation moved into a schoolhouse. A little later he wrote of traveling a thousand miles in three months and someone stealing his horse; "I am now riding an old slug that would wear out a younger man, much less one 68 years old." The Lone Oak Baptist Church was organized by him on the day following the founding of the Brownwood church, whose pastor, the

Reverend Ben Wilson, was to be paid in "meat, meal, potatoes and corn, but would much prefer to have money." In forty years of missionary work Noah T. Byars was never paid more than $500 per annum; almost always his income was well below that figure. His wife and children tended the farm and supported themselves; most early pastors operated in that manner, with the unfortunate consequence of accustoming the laity to the comfortable belief that preachers needed no financial assistance.

Dr. Havins described Byars as a man of slight build, erect, with sharp features, a large nose and penetrating blue eyes. He spoke in a crisp fashion and was never idle. Although in 33 years of ministering to frontier Texans he rode 100,000 miles over roads ranging from poor to non-existent and across (and through) creeks and rivers, unbridged and without ferries, and preached thousands of sermons, and notwithstanding his great contributions to his church, Byars remained acutely conscious of his lack of formal training.

Mrs. Byars died on September 1, 1876, in Hamilton County. He married Mrs. B. J. Moore and became pastor of the First Baptist Church in Brownwood. In his 44 years of missionary effort Byars organized more than sixty churches, including Belton's First Baptist and the First Baptist Church in Corsicana. His last pastorate was at Brown County's Clear Creek Church. Destitute and ill he carried on a mail campaign to establish a college; five years later the Baptists founded Howard Payne College at Brownwood. Byars died in Brownwood July 18, 1888.

Alsatians Settled Castroville

Henri Castro, a Jewish native of Bayonne, France, and a descendant of "Jean de Castro, Viceroy of the Portuguese Indes and Goa," first became interested in Texas as a result of proposals for the settlement of French colonists on the frontier of the Republic. In 1842 Castro visited Texas, and President Houston appointed him consul general to France. He agreed to bring in 600 immigrant families or single men within three years. A family was to receive 640 acres and single men 320 acres, title to pass when a cabin was built and fifteen acres were in cultivation. The Republic was to give Castro one acre for every ten patented to his colonists. Additionally, each colonist promised to convey half the land he received to Castro. Seeking self-reliant people, Castro asked that colonists bring farm implements, tools and sufficient funds to cover their passage and living expenses for one year. The amount was small—an adult's fare for the crossing was only about $30—but substantial for the immigrant, and meeting that requirement demonstrated one's strength, industry and ability to manage. Castro returned to France without seeing the land his colonists would settle.

Most of Castro's colonists were farmers from Alsace, but some were Swiss and Prussian and some were tradesmen and artisans. At least 75% were Catholic. The first 113 set out from Le Havre on the *Ebro* in November, 1842; the voyage required 66 days. In the summer of 1844 Castro arrived in Texas; he had traveled part of the way with Prince Carl, of Solms-Braunfels, who was establishing a colony of Germans. Most of Castro's first 700 colonists got no further than San Antonio and some joined Prince Carl's enterprise. The threat of Mexican invasion and the Indian problem frightened Castro's colonists, who were warned frequently of the hazards of life west of San Antonio. Accompanied by some of Jack Hays' Rangers, Castro inspected his tract in July. Even after Castro promised extra land, the first group to reach the site 25 miles west of San Antonio, on September 3, 1844, included only about thirty of the initial 700 colonists. Rangers were present for Indian protection as the land was surveyed and the buildings were erected.

On September 12 two justices of the peace were elected, the name, Castroville, was chosen, and the Reverend Jean Odin—who would become the first Bishop of Galveston in 1847—laid the cornerstone for the Church of St. Louis. (He signed a certificate to that effect that day, as the "Bishop of Claudiopolis.") There was not then a house between San Antonio and the Rio Grande, and Castroville's church was the only one below Bexar. (In 1840 there were two priests in Texas, both living in San Antonio; when Father Odin arrived there confessions had not been heard for fourteen years.)

Castroville's first parish priest was the Reverend John Gregory Pfanner, an Alsatian who had recruited colonists for Castro. Father Pfanner brought about sixty families with him, mostly from Alsace. Entering through Galveston and Port Lavaca, they arrived in February, 1845, at Castroville, which was, except for Castro's stone house, a collection of mud huts with thatched rooves.

Work on the church stopped soon after it was begun. Father Pfanner devoted himself to land speculation and other activities which led to his indictment for fraud in San Antonio and

The Reverend Claude Dubuis, the priest at Castroville, was a native of France. He became the second Bishop of Texas.

murder in Victoria county. The authors of *St. Louis Church, Castroville*, quoted a letter from Father Odin's assistant, the Reverend John Brands:

> I have been obliged to interdict the priest at Castroville, whose scandalous conduct has not only deserved all the local censure but even the penitentiary; he has set the whole colony of Castro in confusion.

After Father Pfanner's August, 1846, departure for Mexico, Castro—aware that his settlement might fail otherwise—pushed the church to completion. Father Odin dedicated it that November.

In January of 1847, the Reverend Claude Marie Dubuis became the pastor. He and fourteen other priests and seminarians had been recruited in France by Bishop Odin. Father Dubuis and his assistant, the Reverend Matthew Chazelle, of Lyons, were responsible for congregations at Castroville, D'Hanis and Quihi, Castro's Medina County settlements, and for the distant German towns of Fredericksburg and New Braunfels.

The tiny habitation donated by Castro having proved inadequate, the priests built a stone house on the same lot. *St. Louis Church, Castroville* contains this contemporary description of the original:

> Some sticks driven into the ground formed the walls; a little grass made the roof. Neither doors nor windows were necessary, for the whole building was open to the day. A few dozen scorpions, together with myriads of insects, were all the furnishing, if one excepts a rawhide which promised the sleep of a Sybarite.

One day after their house was finished, both priests fell ill with typhoid fever. Father Dubuis survived, but he buried Father Chazelle on September 1, 1847. The Reverend Emmanuel Domenech, Father Chazelle's replacement, had been a seminarian in the immigrant group which had included Father Dubuis.

The colonists had a difficult time. There was much to do in establishing farms. The newcomers had to learn what would grow and how to cultivate it. There was drought and cholera killed many of the settlers in 1849. Indians decapitated a French youth and nailed his head to a tree.

The first church having become too small, Father Domenech went to Louisiana to beg funds for a new one. He returned from his arduous journey sick with malaria and having raised $200. Construction began in early 1850 despite such problems as there not being a single pulley in Castroville. The priests performed much of the labor. Father Dubuis, in January, stood waist-deep in the Medina River so he could cut trees on the bank at the roots and have their full lengths for beams. The priests taught school in the mornings and built the church in the afternoons; it was completed by Easter of 1850.

The two priests barely survived. They drew no salary and took up no regular collections. In his fine thesis Theodore Gittinger told of their meager diet, which included fricasse of cat and alligator. He quoted Father Domenech's account of Father Dubuis' sermon after too much neglect:

> We teach seventy-two of your children, and yet you give nothing, not even for their books. We are about to build a church which will cost you scarcely anything, thanks to our collections, and still you leave us to die of hunger. Call to mind that on one occasion I was not able to preach because I had had no food for forty-eight hours; and that my first colleague, the Abbé Chazelle, died of want still more than of grief.

Father Dubuis promised that should the congregation not provide for them, "tomorrow you will see us no more." The parishioners responded well, but both priests were exhausted. After

This was the first church in Castroville, built by Father Dubuis.

visiting France, Father Domenech was assigned to Brownsville. Father Dubuis spent awhile in New Orleans and then labored alone in Castroville. In 1852 he was succeeded by Franciscans, one of whom, the Reverend Leopold Moczgemba, founded Panna Maria, in Karnes County, the first Polish colony in the new world. In 1859 Benedictines succeeded the Franciscans at Castroville. Father Dubuis became the second bishop of Galveston.

The Reverend Peter Richard, a Frenchman, came to Castroville in 1868. Realizing that the sanctuary was too small for its 226 families, he built the present church, which was first used in 1870. The parsimonious congregation provoked Father Richard into calling it "the most degenerate of the whole diocese and since the inhabitants of Texas are the most immoral in every way, it is useless to look for another parish in America that can surpass Castroville when it comes to wickedness, vulgarity and stupidity."

After the initial hardships were endured Castroville flourished, but when the railroad ignored it, residents began moving to Hondo, which became the seat of Medina County in 1892. John Henry Brown wrote that Henri Castro spent more than $150,000 in his venture; he fed the colonists for a year, and furnished them milk cows, tools, seed and other necessities.

> He was a learned, wise and humane man, unappreciated by many because he was modest and in nowise self-asserting and his tastes were literary. He was a devoted friend of Presidents Lamar, Houston and Jones, all of whom were his friends and did all in their power, each during his term, to advance his great and patriotic idea of planting permanent civilization in Southwest Texas.

Castro did not prosper, for many of his immigrants never settled in his colony. He brought at least 485 families and 457 single men, but only 558 land certificates were sought and issued. Because the state made conveyances directly to the colonists, it was up to Castro to try to get them to deed one half of their land as agreed. The 38,400 acres patented to him constituted his total income from the venture; the land was worth about 10¢ an acre. As the result of a lawsuit he lost most of his property.

Castro was en route to France when he fell ill and died at Monterrey, Mexico, in 1865. Texas ports having been blockaded by the Federals, it was necessary to cross the Rio Grande to obtain passage to Europe. After years of poverty in Castroville, Castro's widow died at San Antonio on February 28, 1871. His son, Lorenzo, died in 1888 without issue.

Henri Castro, born in France, brought .colonists to Texas and founded Castroville, Quihi, Vandenburg, and D'Hanis. He died in Mexico while on his way to France during the Civil War.

St. Louis Church was the third Catholic church built in Castroville.

This window honors the patron saint of Castroville's St. Louis Church.

The Army of Occupation Moved to Corpus Christi

In June of 1845, having been ordered to put his "Army of Observation" in position to enter Texas once annexation was effected, General Zachary Taylor sent his infantry to New Orleans. Texas accepted the American proposal on the fourth of July, and the dragoons left Fort Jesup, Louisiana, over the Camino Real. Taylor's foot soldiers departed New Orleans a few days later; the first contingent, aboard the steamship *Alabama*, arrived at Corpus Christi Bay on July 25. Sandbars made the bay entrance hazardous, so on the following day Taylor landed his men on St. Joseph's Island, 25 miles north of the embryo Corpus Christi, where three or four families lived. The white sand reminded W. S. Henry of Florida:

The fishing here cannot be surpassed; sheep-head, drum, mullet, red-fish, and many others too numerous to mention, abound; the water is literally alive with them . . . . Deer abound. If you are in want of meat, you have but to station yourself behind some of the innumerable sand-hills, near ponds of fresh water.

By hiring fishing boats the troops were moved to the beach beside the village called "Kinney's Ranch" or Corpus Christi. Henry wrote:

The town consists of some twenty or thirty houses, partly situated on a shelf of land, elevated some six or eight feet above the water about two hundred yards broad, and on a bluff which rises from the plain to the height of one hundred feet.

After describing the scene—bounded on the east by the white-caps of the bay, with the Flower Bluffs to the southeast, and westward the plain—Henry reported that it "made one exclaim in the enthusiasm of the moment, 'It is God's favored land—the Eden of America.'" U. S. Grant, not so well-disposed toward Texas, wrote of Corpus Christi:

At the time of its first occupancy by United States troops there was a small Mexican hamlet there, containing probably less than one hundred souls. There was, in addition, a small American trading post, at which goods were sold to Mexican smugglers.

The town had developed from a trading post established in 1838 by Henry Kinney, the only permanent resident and land owner south of the Nueces and therefore a delegate to the annexation convention. He hired as many as fifty men for protection and maintained a couple of artillery pieces. Some Texas Rangers were stationed there also; Peter Bell—later governor and congressman—was their captain. Three of Kinney's men were killed in one skirmish and all were wounded; one survivor had five arrows in his body and had been lanced twice; the Comanche Santa Anna lost seven braves from his war party.

Kinney carried on a heavy trade in illegal goods that had gotten past Mexican customs officers. Traders from below the Rio Grande brought "immense droves of horses and mules, saddles and bridles, Mexican blankets and silver" to exchange for "common unbleached domestics and tobacco." Mexico disapproved of this commerce; one function of Kinney's guards was to protect him from Mexican troops sent to close his operation.

The presence of the troops stimulated Kinney's business and he became the Army quartermaster. His war-time profits enabled Kinney to promote Corpus Christi. In the fifties he sent agents to Europe to bring settlers to his "little Naples," his "Italy of America."

Ulysses S. Grant was a young officer in Zachary Taylor's army, which moved from Fort Jesup, Louisiana, to the beach at Corpus Christi after Texas was annexed.

Kinney's Lone Star Fair at Corpus Christi was Texas' first state fair.

Captain Henry attended mass at the home of an Irishman. The priest, a Spaniard named Esteve, served a 400-mile area. Henry discovered tamales, which he called "themales," and complained of the prevalence of rattlesnakes, which were discovered, two at a time, in the soldiers' tents. On a three-day Nueces River hunting trip, Henry and four others killed ten deer, 51 geese, 18 ducks and a 160-pound panther measuring 7 feet 8 inches from tip of tail to nose.

Troops kept arriving; 251 officers and 3,671 men were camped on the beach by October and Corpus Christi had 2,000 inhabitants, most being "grocery keepers and gamblers, who have come here to feed upon the army." Every kind of building was erected, including a theater accomodating 800 people.

Somewhat to Henry's dismay a legendary mustang, the "White Horse of the Prairies," was captured.

> He was a flea-bitten gray, fourteen hands high, well proportioned, and built a good deal after the pattern of a Conestoga No. 2. His head and neck were really beautiful, perfect Arabian; beautiful ears, large nostrils, great breadth of forehead, and a throttle as large as I have ever seen in a blooded nag. His white mane was two feet long. He looked about twenty-five years old. He was driven into a pen with some hundred others, and lassoed. Thus, by an artifice, was entrapped the monarch of the mustangs . . . .

The troops drilled and paraded endlessly, boosting morale as the men developed pride in their organizations. Jack Hays' Rangers were much admired. Holman Hamilton found this observation in a letter received by Albert Sidney Johnston:

> The feats of horsemanship of our frontier-men are most extraordinary. I saw one of them pick up from the ground three dollars, each fifty yards apart, at full speed, and pass under the horse's neck at a pace not much short of full speed.

The Army numbered about 3,900 by March, 1846, when it moved to the Rio Grande. The last of Taylor's men left Corpus Christi seven months after their arrival, and in spite of his reservations about Texas annexation Lieutenant Grant was proud to be part of the Army of Occupation:

> The men engaged in the Mexican War were brave, and the officers of the regular army, from highest to lowest, were educated in their profession. A more efficient army for its number and armament, I do not believe ever fought a battle . . .

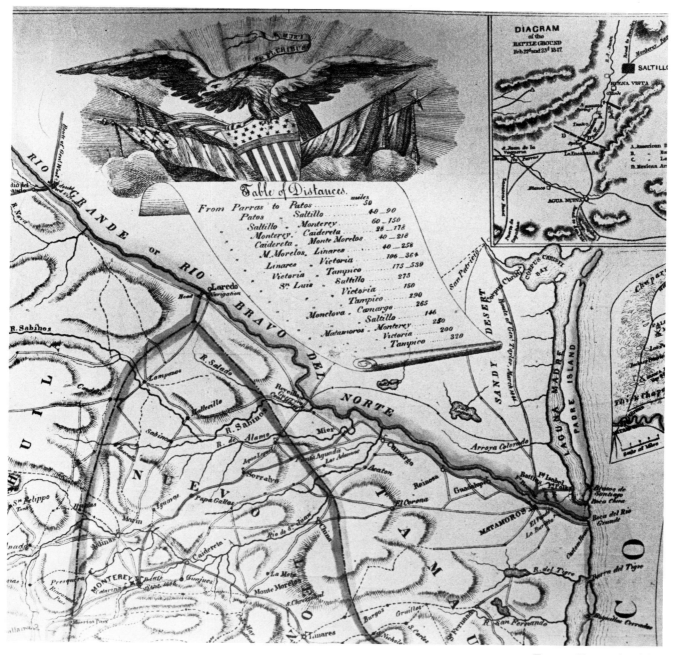

An 1847 map copied from one belonging to General Arista and seized at Resaca de la Palma shows the route of Zachary Taylor's march from Corpus Christi to the Rio Grande.

Fort Brown Was The First Federal Post in Texas

As Texas annexation was concluded Zachary Taylor's Army of Observation moved from Louisiana to become the Army of Occupation at Corpus Christi. Because Mexican officials insisted that Texas had not been lost a decade ago at the Battle of San Jacinto, war was probable. Learning that Mexico was preparing an invasion, in January, 1846, Secretary of War William Marcy ordered the Army of Occupation to the Rio Grande. Taylor was cautioned that hostilities, if any, had to be opened by Mexico.

It was March before Taylor began the march. The command's 307 wagons, 1,900 horses and mules, and 500 teams of oxen required 21 days to cross the 190-mile stretch, of which Lieutenant U. S. Grant recalled: "There was not at that time a single habitation, cultivated field, or herd of domestic animals between Corpus Christi and Matamoras." Map makers named it "the Wild Horse Desert," because of its wilderness state, sandy soil, and mustangs. Grant wrote:

> A few days out from Corpus Christi, the immense herd of wild horses that ranged at that time between the Nueces and the Rio Grande was seen directly in advance of the head of the column and but a few miles off . . . . As far as the eye could reach to our right, the herd extended. To the left, it extended equally. There was no estimating the number of animals in it; I have no idea that they could all have been corralled in the State of Rhode Island, or Delaware, at one time . . . . People who saw the Southern herd of buffalo, fifteen or twenty years ago, can appreciate the size of the Texas herd of wild horses in 1846.

On March 24, as the infantry continued its march to the Rio Grande, Taylor took some cavalry to Point Isabel, where his supply ships were waiting, and began construction of a quartermaster base before rejoining the main column. On the 28th Taylor halted at the border opposite Matamoras; hundreds of Mexicans watched from across the river. Taylor sent word to General Francisco Mexía that his troops were present only to protect American property, but Mexía charged that Taylor's army occupied Mexican soil. (Mexía had earned the admiration of Mier expedition members by refusing to carry out Santa Anna's order to shoot all who escaped at Salado Rancho.) Captain W. S. Henry wrote of their arrival:

> The country passed over was really beautiful; such grazing was never seen before. The ground appeared alive with quail, and every waterhole turned out its flock of ducks . . . . We reached the river at 11 o'clock . . . . Two hours after our arrival a flagstaff was erected, under the superintendence of Colonel Belknap, and soon the flag of our country, a virgin one, was seen floating upon the banks of the Rio Grande, proclaiming in a silent but impressive manner that the "area of freedom" was again extended. As it was hoisted the band of the 8th Infantry played the "Star-Spangled Banner," and the field music "Yankee Doodle."

Only a few houses stood on the south bank of the river; Matamoras was half a mile away. Henry reported: "Our camp was in a cornfield, the corn some six inches high. General Taylor sent for the owner, and told him he would pay him what he thought was the value of the crop."

The site Taylor had chosen was in a bend of the Rio Grande, 33 miles from its mouth. That night the Mexicans mounted a cannon which commanded the American camp; Taylor then

Zachary Taylor assembled at Fort Jesup his Army of Observation. After landing at Corpus Christi it became the Army of Occupation and upon the capture of Matamoras it became the Army of Invasion.

located four cannons so as to "bear directly upon the public square in Matamoras, and within good range for demolishing the enemy." While the earthworks which would become Fort Texas were being built, a thousand yards away the Mexicans raised defensive works.

General Pedro de Ampudia succeeded Mexía on April 12 and demanded an immediate withdrawal beyond the Nueces. Taylor declined. He had the Navy blockade the mouth of the Rio Grande, asked Louisiana for 5,000 volunteers, and requested another 3,000 troops from the Texas governor.

On April 23 President Mariano Paredes y Arrillaga declared a "defensive war" against the United States, and General Mariano Arista, replacing Ampudia, notified Taylor that the two nations were at war. Two American officers had been killed by Mexican guerrillas, but the war really began on April 25 with a battle in which sixteen of Captain Seth Thornton's dragoons were killed and 46 others, including Thornton, were captured by Mexican soldiers.

Taylor hurried to complete his fortification. Fort Texas had earthen walls nine feet high and a ditch fifteen feet deep and twenty feet wide. The perimeter of the fort was 800 yards. Taylor's critics were especially upset about the site; since the river and lagoon surrounded it on three sides there was only one exit. A Taylor subordinate, Colonel E. A. Hitchcock, described it as a cul-de-sac commanding only the river and vulnerable from all sides; he was comforted by a belief that Mexican incompetence was equal to that of Taylor.

Because of concern about his supply line, on May 1 Taylor left Major Jacob Brown and 250 men at Fort Texas while he marched to Point Isabel with about 2,000 troops. Brown, from Massachusetts, had served in the ranks during the War of 1812 prior to receiving his commission. After strengthening defenses at the supply depot, on May 6 Taylor started back to the fort, conscious that a Mexican army twice as large as his own was blocking his path. At Palo Alto and Resaca de la Palma Taylor's army prevailed.

Major Brown's force had been under bombardment since May 3. Learning that Mexican troops were being massed for an assault, on the 5th Brown signalled for help. He was wounded and his leg was amputated that morning. The men voted unanimously to continue the fight despite punishing artillery fire and the enemy's demand for their surrender. Brown died on May 9 while the Battle of Resaca de la Palma was in progress. Casualties were incredibly light at Fort Texas largely due to bomb shelters the men had dug. Sergeant Weigart was killed and thirteen were wounded. Henry wrote:

> The defenders of the fort have suffered everything; they have been harrassed
> night and day, and all looked haggard from the want of sleep . . . . The enemy
> had fired at them some two thousand seven hundred shells and shot . . . .

The outpost was called "Fort Texas" or "Fort Taylor" or "the Camp opposite Matamoras" until it became Fort Brown on May 17.

In June of 1848 construction began on a permanent post a quarter of a mile above the original fort. Officially designated Brownsville Barracks, buildings were constructed from materials salvaged from Army structures at Point Isabel, Brazos Santiago, and Clarksville. Not many troops were stationed at Brownsville after the war, but additional posts were established along the river. Ringgold Barracks opened in October, 1848, and Laredo's Fort McIntosh was occupied in early 1849.

In March, 1859, General David Twiggs closed the post at Brownsville, as well as Fort McIntosh and Ringgold Barracks, to concentrate his troops against the Indians elsewhere. Juan Cortina saw his opportunity. Brownsville was occupied and the flag of Mexico was raised over Fort Brown. By the time Cortina's band was forced away from the Rio Grande in early 1860 the area was devastated. In February of 1861 Twiggs surrendered all Army posts

General David Twiggs commanded the dragoons under Zachary Taylor. When word arrived that the Texans had agreed to annexation, Twiggs brought his men overland from Fort Jesup to Corpus Christi.

to the secessionists, but Fort Brown was not relinquished until March 20, when Confederate colonel John S. Ford assumed command. At least 400 cavalrymen were stationed at Brownsville because of Matamoras' importance to Confederate trade, and Brownsville's population grew from 2,500 to 25,000.

During the American Civil War the small adobe village of Matamoras became a commercial and financial center of perhaps 60,000 residents served by the port of Bagdad, a sleepy old village which suddenly had 15,000 residents. Prior to 1861 half a dozen ships stopped at Bagdad annually, but during the war years 200 to 300 ships were always anchored off Bagdad as cargoes were taken across the sandbars by lighter. Cotton from as far away as Arkansas and Louisiana was hauled across Texas and sold at Matamoras, and the millions of dollars so realized were used to purchase manufactured goods otherwise not available in the South. Matamoras and Bagdad were to the Trans-Mississippi Confederacy what New York was to the North. Richard Marcum's fine dissertation includes this recollection by an old Brownsville citizen:

> Cotton at this time was hauled to the Rio Grande by every type of conveyance from the two-wheeled carts to big wagons holding 25 bales drawn by 50 mules. Cotton could be found stored from Piedras Negras to the mouth of the river, a distance of 300 miles. Cotton roads became established in every direction, and the chaparral was almost white in places from the lint which had blown off passing bales.

After General Nathaniel P. Banks landed about 7,000 Federals at Brazos Santiago on November 2, 1863, General Hamilton Bee burned Fort Brown and destroyed a great quantity of cotton. Military governor A. J. Hamilton tried to function as the state's chief executive from Brownsville, and the Federals stationed as many as 4,000 men in tents at Fort Brown. Except for a small force at Brazos Santiago, Union forces withdrew in July, 1864, as troops were massed for the Red River expedition. Ford's Confederates held Fort Brown until the end of the war.

Fort Brown was rebuilt late in the sixties. Lieutenant W. H. Chatfield wrote in 1890:

> Many changes have occurred since the buildings were first constructed; some have fallen into decay and others have been removed from their original locations, owing to the inroads of the Rio Grande, which now flows over the sites of numerous buildings. The new post was named Fort Brown, after the old work, which, with the prefix of "Old," still withstands a determined seige each recurring practice season, the rampart facing the post being utilized as a bullet-stop, upon which the targets are aligned.

Negotiations to purchase the land were begun prior to the war, but the 385 acres were not conveyed until 1895. For many years burials had been made on the island in the lagoon. In 1909 the remains of Major Brown and 2,800 others were removed to the national cemetery at Alexandria, Louisiana.

It is not clear why the reservation was purchased, for Fort Brown was the Army's most unhealthy post. The lagoon was simply a stagnant pool fed by surface water from the fort and cemetery. A medical officer, noting that 58% of the soldiers were on sick report for malaria, stated: "The washed out appearance of nearly every soldier in the command plainly showed the unhealthy surroundings . . . . If this unwholesome spot must be occupied I can only recommend that the garrison be reduced to the minimum and entirely changed every year." In the following year 286 malaria cases were recorded, an average of almost two for each man at the fort.

During the long reign of Porfírio Diaz there was little work for the garrison since the

Mexican dictator was reasonably effective in keeping the peace. In 1906 someone randomly fired more than a hundred rounds in Brownsville, killing one man and wounding a policeman, and black soldiers of the 25th Infantry at Fort Brown were accused of the raid. On November 9 President Theodore Roosevelt discharged dishonorably the regiment's enlisted men because no one in the outfit would identify the guilty parties.

Fort Brown was closed and was not again used by the Army until 1914, when troops were sent to the border because of the revolution in Mexico.

After Pancho Villa's 1916 raid on Columbus, New Mexico, the post grew in importance, as 150,000 soldiers and national guardsmen were stationed on the Rio Grande. Fort Brown was a cavalry post from 1917 until its closing in May, 1944; the United States Army's last horse cavalry brigade served there. In 1948 the front 162 acres were conveyed to the City of Brownsville. Fort Brown Memorial Center stands on that site. The old post hospital, deeded to the school district, is occupied by Texas Southmost College.

Commanding officers of Fort Brown included Ranald Mackenzie, the Indian fighter, J. J. Reynolds, who commanded Texas during reconstruction, and Abner Doubleday, the inventor of baseball.

American Blood Was Shed on American Soil

On April 10, 1846, Colonel Truman Cross, Zachary Taylor's assistant quartermaster general, rode out of Fort Texas and did not return. A dozen days later his body was recovered; Romano Falcon had killed him with a blow from a pistol butt. After a formal military funeral, Cross was buried at the foot of the flag pole at Fort Texas. Lieutenant Theodoric Porter, while on a patrol, was killed by bandits on April 19; his body was never found. In that neither casualty was inflicted by Mexican soldiers no act of war had occurred.

From the beginning General Taylor was uneasy about the distance—33 miles—separating his supply depot at Point Isabel and Fort Texas. Reports that large numbers of Mexican troops had crossed the river made it necessary that he determine whether his line of communication was intact. Taylor sent Captain Seth B. Thornton and 62 dragoons to ascertain the location and intentions of the invaders, and on April 25 at Carricitos Ranch, about 28 miles from Fort Texas, Thornton blundered into a force of 1,600 Mexican soldiers commanded by General Anastasio Torrejón. Sixteen Americans were killed, and except for one released as a messenger, the others were taken prisoner. Thornton, at first thought to be dead, was only stunned when his wounded horse, which "had carried him through the Florida war," fell on him. The prisoners were exchanged after a few days, but the war had begun.

Adolphus Glaevecke had a personal version of the skirmish:

> The officers stopped at my ranch for information, as they had done on several occasions, and I fixed them up a good meal, including eggs, which were a luxury they seldom enjoyed. I told them there were 9,000 Mexican troops on this side of the river, and they would have to be very careful or they would fall into an ambush. They went on up the river, and on the following day, the whole command was surrounded and captured near Carricitos' Ranch, where they had sought shelter in a deserted house from a heavy rain-storm which had suddenly overtaken them. Ten men were killed in trying to escape. The officers and about fifty men were exchanged later. I picked up a horse pistol on the scene of the capture, and that was the only thing the Mexicans didn't get.

Sam Bell Maxey quoted Taylor's message: "An engagement has taken place between a detachment of our cavalry and the Mexicans in which we were worsted . . . . so war has actually commenced." On May 11 President James K. Polk reported to Congress that Mexico had "shed American blood on American soil." Congress appropriated $10 million and authorized the recruitment of 50,000 volunteers. War was declared on the 13th after a vote of 142 to 11 in the House and 40 to 2 in the Senate.

Here "American blood was shed on American soil" as Mexican troops killed 16 Americans and captured the rest of Captain Seth Thornton's command.

Taylor Prevailed at Palo Alto and Resaca De La Palma

Because Fort Polk, the quartermaster depot at Point Isabel, was 33 miles away, Fort Texas was in constant danger of being cut off from supplies and reinforcements. To keep Taylor informed on the situation former Texas Ranger captain Samuel Walker located the base camp of his scouting company on Palo Alto Lake, midway between the two posts. On April 28, 1846, Mexicans overran Walker's camp, killing six and capturing four of his men. In response to Walker's warning that the enemy was crossing the river in force, on May 1 Taylor led 2,000 troops toward the Gulf to intercept the Mexicans and strengthen the supply depot.

Taylor improved the Point Isabel defenses and assembled a supply wagon for Major Jacob Brown and the men at Fort Texas. Aware that General Mariano Arista's army stood between him and the fort, Taylor began the return march on the afternoon of May 7. Telling his men, who numbered 2,228 by virtue of reinforcements acquired at Fort Polk, that the Mexicans controlled the road and that a battle was probable, Taylor promised victory if they followed his instructions. The infantry was reminded that "their main dependence must be in the bayonet." In that Taylor was mistaken, for the Battle of Palo Alto turned out to be an artillery duel.

After covering about seven miles the Americans made camp. The march was continued on the morning of May 8. Years later U. S. Grant recalled:

> Formerly the river ran by Resaca de la Palma, some four or five miles east of the present channel. The old bed of the river at Resaca had become filled at places, leaving a succession of little lakes. The timber that had formerly grown upon both banks, and for a considerable distance out, was still standing. This timber was struck six or eight miles out from the beseiged garrison, at a point known as Palo Alto—"Tall trees" or "woods."

In open prairie the Mexican line extended for a mile and a half, crossing the road to Fort Texas. Taylor halted a mile away and formed his army. The men were sent, half at a time, to fill their canteens.

As the Americans closed to within 700 yards, the Mexican artillery began an ineffective fire. Taylor halted, deployed the infantry, and opened up with his batteries. Captain Henry wrote that Ringgold's guns:

> told with deadly effect upon their mass of cavalry; platoons appeared to be mowed down at a time. The two eighteen-pounders carried death and destruction with them. The cavalry soon found it was getting too warm for them and commenced moving off . . . and were tickled into a gallop by a discharge of the eighteens.

Duncan's battery was equally accurate. The devastatingly precise American fire was demoralizing to Arista's troops, many of whom were Indians, forced into the army, untrained, underfed, and ill-equipped.

Having intended an attack, Arista had placed General Anastasio Torrejón's 1,000 mounted lancers in front of the infantry, but as the deadly cannonade began he did not order a

This painting of Palo Alto was done within months of the May 8, 1846 battle. General Taylor had expected an infantry action, but instead an artillery duel resulted after the army of General Arista blocked the road to Fort Texas.

charge and his men were slaughtered by the accuracy of the batteries. The Mexican artillery was doing little damage; the range was often short, and the Americans simply jumped the rolling iron balls. Finally Arista ordered Torrejón's lancers forward, but they attacked in column rather than in line and were halted by Taylor's infantry while Ringgold turned his batteries on them.

As the lancers retreated, the prairie caught fire. The burning tall grass yielded a heavy curtain of smoke which made it impossible for the armies to see each other. The Mexicans were flanked, forcing them to change their line of battle and creating confusion. After four hours of fighting, the armies made camp. American casualties were five dead—including Samuel Ringgold—43 wounded, and two missing. Henry recalled, "The wounds of the men were very severe, most of them requiring amputation of some limb. The surgeon's saw was going the livelong night, and the groans of the poor sufferers were heartrending." Officially Mexican casualties were 252, but after visiting the field the next morning Henry estimated enemy losses at 500 and concluded, "The great disproportion in the loss of the two armies arose from this fact: We fired at their masses; they at our batteries." According to Sam Bell Maxey, "It was a fair field, an open fight, and odds three to one in numbers on the enemy's side, but victory perched on our banner." Henry wrote: "General Taylor ordered our parties in every direction to search for the wounded of the enemy, had them brought in, and attended to with the same care as our men."

On the next morning the Mexican army marched toward Fort Texas but halted about five miles away at the Resaca de la Guerra, just north of the Resaca de la Palma. Maxey described the rough site as "Ground cut up by ravines and covered with chaparral." The fighting would resemble that Taylor had predicted for Palo Alto; the broken terrain would afford protection against artillery and require Taylor's outnumbered infantry and cavalry to penetrate the dense brush and find an enemy with embankments for cover. The chaparral was composed of mesquite, prickly pear, and vines so dense as to be almost impenetrable. Natural paths led to prairie sometimes, but more often they simply stopped in the chaparral; a stranger could not find his way through the chaparral, which came within a mile of the site later occupied by Brownsville's city market.

The Americans halted at noon and moved out an hour later. Once again the enemy commanded the road. Henry said:

> The enemy occupying the opposite bank of a river, concave toward us, had planted their batteries to rake the road, and every approach (few in number) through the almost impenetrable chaparral. The fire of the enemy was drawn by the advance. Lieutenant Ridgely, fit successor to the gallant Ringgold, was ordered forward with his battery. The struggle for victory then commenced. The artillery of the enemy swept the ground with their grape and cannister; Lieutenant Ridgely returned it with murderous effect. Masses of their Infantry, lining the banks of the ravine, and pressed forward into the chaparral, were met by our skirmishers on the left with a gallantry and determination, on both sides, rarely equaled. Repeatedly were bayonets crossed, the enemy giving way slowly, and fighting for every inch of the ground . . . . Owing to the dense chaparral, the Regiments became mixed, but fought not the less severely.

Captain May led his men across the ravine and captured the battery. All the fighting was to the left of the road, for on the right:

> The density of the chaparral was such that they could not make their way through, but were forced to return, in order to get into the action. They reached the ravine just after the desperate charge of the Infantry . . . had completely routed the enemy . . . . The enemy was in full retreat. On we pushed, hemmed in

a narrow road by a dense chaparral on each side, the artillery advancing and pouring in its bloody fire, and clearing the road.

Taylor was in the middle of the action, but Arista remained in his tent composing a report on the battle of Palo Alto. A Mexican cannon was covering the road effectively until it was captured and turned on the Mexican infantry, which bolted. Taylor reported, "Bayonet to bayonet, and sword to sword, we completely routed them."

The Americans pursued the enemy to the Rio Grande, and many soldiers drowned trying to cross. Henry announced:

> Our brave general had gained a glorious victory over the best-appointed army Mexico ever sent into the field; confident of success, in an almost impregnable position, and with an overwhelming force, at least three to one. There were two thousand troops not in the battle of the 8th, who crossed the river the evening of that day, expressly to join in the battle of the 9th . . . . History does not furnish a more striking battle than "Resaca de la Palma," the battle of the 9th of May.

The American loss was 33 dead and 89 wounded. While Arista reported 160 dead, 228 wounded and 159 missing, others estimated Mexican casualties at 2,000. Arista's baggage and papers were seized; a general and colonel were captured along with 2,000 stands of arms and 150,000 rounds of ammunition.

Five days after Congress delcared war, on May 13, 1846, Taylor's "Army of Invasion" occupied Matamoras without opposition.

Charles Stillman Founded Brownsville

At sixteen Connecticut-born Charles Stillman went to sea aboard a ship belonging to his father, who traded in Mobile, New Orleans and Matamoras. Charles Stillman came to Texas in February of 1828, landing at Brazos Santiago, the seaport serving Matamoras. Ocean-going vessels unloaded at Brazos Santiago, from whence cargo was taken by shallow-draft vessels 25 miles up the Rio Grande to Matamoras. While still a boy Stillman traded in Durango and took up residence in Matamoras, where he worked for his father, importing lumber and manufactured goods and exporting wool, hides, and silver.

Founded early in the 19th century, Matamoras was named for Mariano Matamoras, a priest and general who lost his life in Mexico's war of independence; the town was originally called the Congregation of Refugio. Five years after Mexico became independent, the governor of Tamaulipas declared that "to perpetuate the memory of one of the martyrs of the country" the town would be called Villa de Matamoras. The Mexican Congress honored the city for "its heroic defense against the traitors who assaulted it" in 1851; in the council chamber at the Matamoras city hall the wall behind the mayor's chair was painted in large gold letters "Invincible and Heroic Matamoras, October 31, 1851." All documents, public and private from that time on referred to the city as "H. Matamoras."

Stillman was a Matamoras merchant during the Texas Revolution and the Mexican War. In March, 1846, Zachary Taylor built an earthwork across the Rio Grande from Matamoras which became Fort Brown after Major Jacob Brown was killed there in an artillery battle. When General Pedro Ampudia ordered Americans in Matamoras to relocate in the City of Victoria, Stillman went into hiding and did not emerge until Taylor occupied Matamoras.

Believing the area adjoining Fort Brown would make a desirable townsite because of the international boundary and interest in the Rio Grande stimulated by the war, in August of 1848 Stillman hired George Lyons and S. P. Gelston to survey and plat 4,676 acres as the City of Brownsville. One factor favoring the location was the presence of Fort Brown, which attracted commerce and then people and spent government money; another important consideration was that Brazos Santiago was on the Texas side of the river and would serve the new town as it had Matamoras. William Neale, an Englishman who arrived on the Rio Grande in 1834, stated:

> Brazos Santiago was then a fine harbor in which twenty vessels could ride at anchor, and swing with the tide without interfering with each other, while now all ships have to be moored to prevent them from striking on one of the numerous bars and shoals which have been formed by the silt of more than half a century.

On the Brownsville site there was not then a habitation of any kind. When Taylor came in 1846, Neale recalled:

> . . . there were not more than a dozen jacales scattered about this vicinity among the fields of cotton and corn. Wild horses and cattle roamed over the whole country and Indians were as thick as blackbirds, and quite as saucy.

Charles Stillman, the founder of Brownsville, built this house on Washington Street. His son, James Stillman, born here, became president of the First City National Bank in New York City and built a fortune of some $200 million.

In Stillman's Brownsville, streets commemorated presidents Washington, Adams, Jefferson, Madison, Monroe, and Jackson; Elizabeth Street honored his fiancee, Saint Francis was for his father, who died in 1838, and Saint Charles Street he named for himself. Neale, in his 1876 oration on the occasion of the American Centennial, outlined the history of Brownsville, which originally possessed many of the characteristics of a no-mans land:

> I believe more men of desperate character, desperate fortunes, and evil propensities were congregated here on this frontier from 1846 to 1848, than ever got together in any other place. When I say any other place, of course, I mean *on earth*, since the deluge.

Neale testified to the truth of the proverb which teaches:

> "As sure as the devil sends a poison so sure Providence provides an antidote!" Our antidote for this great moral poison was the gold of California. That exodus purged society and carried off most of the desperadoes; the few that remained here among us, as is usual with them, killed off one another and from that time the history of Brownsville as a civilized community may be dated.

In late 1848 Stillman and Samuel Belden, his partner, were each building brick stores on the townsite; Brownsville became the seat of Cameron County that December. Lots sold for $300 apiece, but there were title difficulties, and a cholera epidemic early in 1849 took a heavy toll. Other problems included the continual revolutionary activity across the river. The population was 4,000, by the estimate of John S. Ford, when Brownsville was incorporated in 1850, but at secession the town had only half that number of citizens.

Stillman married, in Connecticut, Elizabeth Goodrich and took her to his home on Washington Street in Brownsville. James Stillman was born there in 1850 and Isabel Stillman two years later. Mrs. Stillman took the children to Connecticut in 1853 and never returned, but Charles Stillman remained on the Rio Grande, going north to visit his wife each summer except during the Civil War.

In 1857 Brownsville suffered a disastrous fire. Neale said:

> Our city in those days was an arsenal where the revolutionists of Mexico obtained considerable supplies of arms and munitions of war. In nearly every store, kegs of powder were piled on the shelves with groceries or dry goods.

The store where the fire began was next door to Stillman's brick building. It housed 300 kegs of powder, which exploded.

> None of the persons who were within those premises were ever seen again, except one, a clerk, who was seen amidst the fire and ruin, apparently blind, staggering and groping against a side wall of the store. He was rescued, and recovered from his terrible injuries.

The number of lives lost was never determined, but the city council passed an ordinance limiting the quantity of powder one might possess.

Stillman invested in a number of ventures, including several ranches and a Rio Grande steamboating partnership with Mifflin Kenedy and Richard King. In 1862 Stillman was running 12,000 head of cattle on the Rancho Los Laureles, which he sold to Kenedy in 1868.

During the Civil War Brownsville flourished as great quantities of cotton were hauled across Texas for sale in Matamoras. When Confederate general Hamilton P. Bee abandoned Brownsville he set fire to Fort Brown and to the cotton awaiting transport. Neale's journal reflects how on November 3, 1863, the general and his staff had dinner at Henry Miller's place, then advised Miller to hire as many carts as possible and take what he wanted from Fort Brown's commissary to cover their bill, for they had no money with which to pay him. Neale wrote:

They went into the garrison pretty high from the effects of the champagne, and orders were immediately given to fire the quarters. The order was obeyed, and all the buildings except two were soon enveloped in flames. I hurried my wife and children to the ferry, to pass them over the river for safety.

Some of the homes in town caught fire but citizens managed to save Brownsville. Colonel James Fremantle, of the British Coldstream Guards, in 1863 deemed it "about the rowdiest town of Texas, which was the most lawless state in the Confederacy."

Stillman moved to Matamoras before the Federals took Brownsville. His steamships were registered in Matamoras and he owned real estate and kept as much personal property as possible there. He moved north in 1866 and died in New York City on December 18, 1875. The only one of his six children to marry was James Stillman, who was president of the National City Bank of New York from 1891 to 1908 and left an estate of some $200 million; two of his children married Rockefellers and one a Whitney; a grandchild married a Carnegie.

Juan Cortina Captured Brownsville

The establishment of Fort Brown, the first permanent post of the United States Army in Texas, across the Rio Grande from Matamoras attracted settlers and caused a substantial trade to develop. Business was stimulated by the California gold rush, as forty-niners came by water to Brazos Santiago and Brownsville and traveled overland to the Pacific. By the end of its first decade Brownsville had about 3,000 residents, including a substantial population of outlaws and riff-raff common to any frontier.

One of the badmen was Juan Nepomuceno Cortina, born of a good family in Camargo, on May 16, 1824. About five feet eight inches tall, he weighed 170 pounds and had red hair and green eyes. Cortina's mother owned about 44,000 acres west of Brownsville, and his brother, José, was the tax collector of Cameron County. "Cheno" Cortina had a good mind but did badly in school; John S. Ford stated: "He never remained many days under a teacher without beating some boy terribly and getting himself expelled. He attained manhood without being able to read or write." A soldier in Arista's army when Zachary Taylor established Fort Brown, Cortina drew to him "men of wild, and in many instances, dissolute habits," for he "understood his countrymen of the lower classes."

Cortina's bandit career was long and bloody. Indicted in Cameron County for murder about 1850, he made himself scarce until the witnesses disappeared. Cortina was charged with horse theft and robbery but was never tried. Later indictments did not keep him out of Brownsville, where he appeared armed and accompanied by henchmen.

In February of 1859 General David Twiggs withdrew the troops from the Rio Grande for Indian duty in northwest Texas, leaving unprotected 250 miles of border, from the Gulf to Laredo. Fort Brown's closing jeopardized the very existence of Brownsville, although Twiggs assured his superiors that there was no danger of trouble in the valley, an odd claim, for he knew better. He had spent many years in Texas, had, in fact, led Taylor's dragoons from Fort Jesup, Louisiana, to the Fort Brown site. William Neale described what happened after the troops were gone: "This section was then ripe for development, but the bane of the border, Cortina, touched it with his poisoned wand, and left only a blackened and scarred semblance of its former beauty." In 1877 Sam Bell Maxey told the United States Senate:

> The country had been growing wealthy in the productive industry of raising cattle, but in 1859 a new character appeared on the Mexican side who has been from 1859 down to this present good hour the pest and the curse of the border, Juan Nepomuceno Cortina, the great leader and chieftain of the border marauders, who has caused the loss of millions of dollars of property and of hundreds of lives of Texans as shown by the evidence.

On July 13, 1859, City Marshal Robert Shears was in the process of arresting a man for creating a disturbance when Cortina tried to intervene. Shears ignored Cortina, who fired twice, wounding the marshal in the shoulder. Cortina mounted his horse, swung the rescued man up behind him, and shouting threats and boasting about what he would do should anyone try to interfere, he rode out of Brownsville and across the river.

Cortina was hailed as a hero by all who disliked Americans. His bandit gang fell upon the

Bandit leader Juan Cortina was the bane of the border country for decades.

Rio Grande country, killing and taking what they wanted. Other badmen followed suit; Ford stated: "This gave an invitation to the desperadoes, cutthroats, and robbers of that region to kill and plunder the unfortunate residents . . . ."

Although September 16 is the anniversary of Mexican independence, the 1859 celebration was deferred to the 27th; on that evening many Brownsville residents took part in the festivities at Matamoras. Neale wrote:

> . . . consequently, on the morning of the 28th, when Cortina, with a band of about 200 ruffians, commenced his murderous raid, many persons who were awakened by the shouting and shooting in the streets, thought that it was merely over-jolly parties who were returning from the ball given in Matamoras . . . . This idea prevented many, who would have been among the first to go to the defense of the city, from getting up, for the raid commenced just at the break of day and our citizens were not aware of their situation until they were all completely at the mercy of the ruffians, who were well organized and drilled, for immediately on entering the city, horsemen well mounted stood guard at every corner of the streets and would not permit any two men to join company.

Of those who were celebrating in Matamoras, Ford recalled:

> When they returned to the American side of the river, they were astonished to find the country in the possession of Cortina, who was more celebrated for lawlessness than for anything else. Everything was at his mercy. He and his followers killed whomever they wished, robbed whomever they pleased. They intended to finish their diabolical work by burning the city.

Cortina vowed to kill the Americans—only about 100 Brownsville citizens were not of Mexican extraction—but promised not to harm others. Many fled. "They broke open the county jail, liberated and armed the prisoners with arms they had stolen from other places . . . . They left four gory victims stark dead, of our citizens," said Neale, whose son was murdered in his bed.

Shouting "Viva Cortina!" and "Mueran los gringos!" (Death to Americans!) they raised the Mexican flag over the abandoned fort. William Johnson, the jailer, took refuge in Vivian Garcia's house: Cortina's men killed both. Constable George Morris was murdered. After two days Cortina withdrew, having been persuaded to do so by a kinsman and by Mexican general José Carbajal. For $100,000 and delivery of his enemies, Cortina offered to leave Brownsville alone. Cameron County's plight was explained by Neale:

> At that time we had not a State or Federal soldier on this frontier, nor any organized militia. In vain we called for aid. For months during that winter, every man of us, young or old, had to go, not an hour or two, but all night and every night, into the barricades. Cortina had us closely beseiged, and his men would fire on us every night during the darkest hours, from the outskirts of the city.
> Cortina's forces were daily augmented from the other side of the river. His fame spread, and hundreds of the riff-raff and scum of the Northern States of Mexico, swarmed down on this frontier, and they have never since returned to their native haunts.

Mifflin Kenedy and Francisco Yturria posted guards. Some of General Carbajal's troops from Matamoras were hired to defend Brownsville, which was cut off from the outside world. The bandits intercepted incoming and outgoing mail. When William Tobin's Rangers hanged one of the outlaws, Cortina threatened to level Brownsville. Major Samuel Heintzelman arrived on December 5, 1859, and reported: "There is not an American, or any property belonging to an American that could be destroyed" or carried away in the 120-mile strip from Brownsville to Rio Grande City.

The Cameron County grand jury reported:

> that from the fact that Cortinas and all them with him were Mexican by birth—most of them also by residence—and . . . from the further fact that said Cortinas had been for nearly three months a fugitive from the pursuit of justice residing in Mexico, but more especially from the cries of "Viva la Republica Mexicana," and . . . from the efforts on his part, unavailing for the want of proper tackle, to raise the flag of Mexico upon the flag-staff in the center of the parade ground . . . the entry upon the city of Brownsville, on the 28th of September, 1859, was an invasion of American territory by armed Mexicans under the Mexican flag . . . .

Cortina's band had grown to perhaps 800 men. Through the efforts of Ford's Rangers and Heintzelman's soldiers Cortina was checked. After a costly defeat on December 27 Cortina crossed the river and began raising another band.

In early 1860 the steamboat *Ranchero*, belonging to Richard King and Mifflin Kenedy, was to take $300,000 in specie from Rio Grande City to Brownsville. Cortina, with 300 men, intended to capture the boat at La Bolsa bend, about 35 miles above Brownsville. Ford's 48 Rangers dispersed the attackers. One Ranger was killed, while Cortina lost 29 dead and 40 wounded. Dismayed by Cortina's escape, Ford complained:

> Cortina was the last to leave the field. He faced his pursuers, emptied his revolver, and tried to halt his panic-stricken men . . . . One shot struck the cantle of his saddle, one cut a lock of hair from his head, a third cut his bridle rein, a fourth passed through his horse's ear, and a fifth struck his belt. He galloped off, unhurt.

Lieutenant Colonel Robert E. Lee, assigned to Texas, set out from San Antonio, on March 15, 1860, to disperse the bandits. From Eagle Pass he traveled down the river, conferring with Mexican officials at every point. Ford's Rangers and Captain George Stoneman's cavalry pursued Cortina's men forty miles into Mexico, making the valley safe for awhile, but Cortina's continuing agitation against the United States and avoidance of punishment encouraged other border bandits.

Cortina was a general in the Mexican Army and governor of Tamaulipas during the American Civil War. He was mayor of Matamoras in 1875, but when General Porfírio Diaz sought help for his revolution in Brownsville the next year, citizens donated conditioned upon Cortina's being kept away from the Rio Grande. Cortina's half brother reportedly gave $50,000. After Diaz became president, the military governor of Tamaulipas, General Servando Canales, arrested Cortina, tried him, and sentenced him to death. For some reason John Ford urged clemency. Cortina was required to spend the rest of his life in Mexico City. He died October 30, 1894, was given a military funeral and buried in the Panteón de Dolores.

Boehm Led Mackenzie's Tonkawa Scouts

Peter M. Boehm joined the Second Cavalry as a private in 1858. During the Civil War he was General George A. Custer's bugler, and at the battle of Gettysburg, during the charge of Michigan's Wolverine brigade, Boehm sabered and captured General Wade Hampton's bugler. (Hampton suffered a facial cut also.) Impressed by his boldness, Custer obtained a commission for Boehm and made him an aide. Boehm won the Congressional Medal of Honor at Dinwiddie Courthouse and was badly wounded at the battle of Five Forks.

After the war First Lieutenant Boehm, assigned to Colonel Ranald S. Mackenzie's Fourth Cavalry, was given charge of the Tonkawa scouts. Because the task required a special flair, and in order to afford easy identification during battle, Mackenzie allowed Boehm to wear a wide-brimmed, low-crowned white sombrero instead of the regulation hat. Captain R. G. Carter wrote: "We all envied that hat. It was softer, cooler and more comfortable than our black campaign hats." When the other officers wanted similar headgear, Mackenzie snapped, "No! Boehm is in command of the Indians. As such he is outside the marching column, a sort of 'free lance,' and somewhat of an independent and picturesque character." Carter said, "We never saw Boehm go sailing by with his miscellaneous bunch of Ton-ka-way Indians . . . that we did not sigh and almost bark our disappointment and disapproval of his un-uniform head covering flapping in the breeze . . . ."

The scouts lived in the Flat below Fort Griffin. The Tonkawa furnished their own horses, and the Army provided guns, ammunition, and rations. Fine warriors, they hated the Comanche, who had helped them become a small tribe verging on extinction.

In September of 1871, Mackenzie left Camp Cooper with about 600 men for a Panhandle campaign. "The Indian scouts, our faithful 'Tonks,' under Lieutenant P. M. Boehm, were far in advance, well fanned out, combing the country for trails," Carter wrote. He described their preparations for meeting Quanah Parker's Comanche near present Crosby County:

The Ton-ka-ways—McCord, the head chief; Simoon, "One-armed Charlie," Jesse, Lincoln, Grant, "Old Henry," Anderson, Job, William, Buffalo (the "Beau Brummel" of the "Tonks") . . . slipped from their riding animals, caught up, from their pony herd being driven on the flank, their favorite war ponies, until then unused, stripped all superfluous loads from their saddles, and quickly began, in their rude, inartistic way, to paint and adorn their persons for the coming battle, which we now surely considered was impending. A small piece of looking glass, a puddle of saliva in the hollow of the hand, much red, green, yellow, and black paint (ochre), were quickly mixed and applied in reeking daubs. The cream, claybank, dun or white pony was plentifully striped. Headdresses, horns, much red flannel, and bright-colored feathers completed the "Tonk" ensemble. The whole operation did not exceed five minutes, but sufficiently long to excite the laughter of the entire column of brave troops even at the critical moment, when all were expecting a battle. Our gallant allies then pranced alongside the column, posturing, moving their heads from side to side, brandishing their carbines, and evidently feeling all the pride of conquering monarchs, so self-conscious were they of the dignity which all this display of paint, feathers, gew-gaws, etc., gave them.

Lieutenant Peter Boehm commanded Ranald Mackenzie's Tonkawa scouts in the campaign against the Comanche on the Plains.

Next day the soldiers killed two Comanche braves; after shooting some bullets into the bodies, the Tonkawa scalped them "ears and all," cut pieces of skin for their medicine bags, and held a scalp dance when they got back to Fort Griffin. The Tonkawa were fearless except at night in strange country, for they feared the soldiers might mistake them for Comanche.

Relations between Boehm and his charges were not always peaceful. While pursuing Kicking Bird earlier in 1871, McCord, the Tonkawa chief, complained to Mackenzie that "Bim" withheld their rations. Boehm explained that upon receiving three-days rations the scouts would immediately consume it; two days later he could not find them because they were out hunting for something to eat. McCord snapped, "Oh him, Bim—he heap lie; he heap go to H--L; him heap D--n--!" Mackenzie then explained that three "lations" had to last "three suns." Finally because of his great regard for Mackenzie, McCord smiled and forgave Boehm.

In Blanco Canyon, north of present Crosbyton, Quanah had Carter and his men in a dangerous position when suddenly the Comanche pulled away, frightened by the approach of Boehm and "all of our Ton-ka-way Indians, with Texas, the squaw, fantastically arrayed in all their finery . . . ." Although Mackenzie had ordered the squaws left at home, Texas was "mounted on a claybank pony which she had striped with paint so that it closely resembled a zebra, and decorated with feathers and red flannel, was now in the midst of the bucks, full of fight, yelling and screaming like a demon—a veritable virago." In his account of the battle which followed, Carter wrote of the Comanche:

> In the rear of the Indian lines could be seen the squaws now bringing up led ponies, keeping up their shrill, discordant screeching and screaming, and at the base of the butte, or low mountain, the savages were spread out, and circling here and there, looked like a swarm of angry bees, so that it was almost impossible to estimate the number of the moving mass with any accuracy, although we judged that there might have been from three hundred to four hundred—including the squaws.
>
> They were heartily responding to the shouts and war whoops of our scouts, sometimes interlarded with most emphatic and regular old-fashioned, round cursing. Here the real excitement and fascinating charm, so peculiar to an Indian fight, began. It was one grand, but rather dangerous, circus. As before stated, an irregular line of battle, or front, was kept up, always, however, in continual motion, every individual warrior fighting for himself—each, as he came around on the front arc of his right or left hand circle, whooping, or yelling, and brandishing his arms. This yell can hardly be described . . . .
>
> At no time did our lines approach close rifle distance. Occasionally a Ton-ka-way would leave his circle, and, dashing straight to the front, would be imitated by a Comanche, both apparently bent upon meeting in personal combat, or a duel; but, as we breathlessly watched, expecting every moment to see the collision, they whirled and delivered their fire, strongly reinforced by untranslatable Indian language—which we took to be serious name-calling—they darted back to their places in the ever-changing battle line.
>
> This went on for some time. Occasionally a warrior could be seen to stagger as though about to fall; again, a pony was shot and fell, but instantly the wounded savage was hurried to the rear to be cared for by the squaws, who also brought up an extra pony, to remount the one whose animal had been shot, not forgetting to keep up their ear-splitting screaming, horrible screeching, and noisy exhibition of courage.

Peter Boehm, promoted to captain in 1873, retired as a major on March 1, 1876. He died in 1914 and was buried in Chicago. Carter had his body moved to Arlington National Cemetery where "on each Memorial Day he plants a flag over his grave in loving remembrance of this gallant soul and generous, faithful companion."

Some Tonkawa dance in the Indian Territory "before the beginning of a rain storm" in 1901.

The Fourth Cavalry Invaded Mexico

The Kickapoo in Mexico had so harassed Texans living along the Rio Grande that in 1872 the Congress of the United States sent commissioners to investigate. The American consul in Piedras Negras explained: "So long as the Kickapoo have the protection of the Mexican Government and cross into Texas to loot, rob, and plunder, and as long as these acts are countenanced by the citizens of Mexico, and as long as the Kickapoo can find a ready market for their booty, they will never willingly quit." Convinced that Mexican authorities would provide no protection to the residents of the border country the commission recommended removal of the Kickapoo to the Indian Territory.

As raids continued General William T. Sherman transferred General Ranald S. Mackenzie and his Fourth Cavalry Regiment—perhaps the best in the Army—to Fort Clark from Fort Richardson in March of 1873. Secretary of War William Belknap and General Philip Sheridan arrived at Fort Clark on April 11. Sheridan instructed Mackenzie to stop the raids by attacking the Indian villages in Mexico; Carter quoted Sheridan's exhortation to "let it be a campaign of annihilation, obliteration and complete destruction." To Mackenzie's request for orders, Sheridan pounded the table and shouted, "Damn the orders! Damn the authority! You are to go ahead on your own plan of action, and your authority and backing shall be General Grant and myself."

The possible consequences of leading troops across an international boundary without written orders worried Mackenzie, but evidently he never hesitated. He confided the mission to Adjutant R. G. Carter, Ike Cox, the guide at Fort Clark, and half-Indian scouts Green Van and Art McLain, whose ranches the Indians had raided. The guide and scouts rode into Mexico to determine the best route to the villages while Mackenzie was accumulating supplies and having the horses shod. His order to grind the sabers to "a razor edge" aroused comment since "we had never, thus far, carried such encumbrances as sabres on an ordinary Indian Campaign." Preparations were made quietly; some residents of Bracketville—deemed by Carter "the exact counterpart of Jacksboro, near Fort Richardson, the ulcer of every garrison, an inevitable fungus growth"—might warn the hostiles.

Acting upon information that most of the warriors were away from the villages, on May 17, 1873, elements of the regiment met at Las Moras Creek. About 2 p.m. six companies and twenty Seminole Negro scouts commanded by First Lieutenant John Bullis—nearly 400 men—descended the Las Moras to the Rio Grande. After explaining their mission, Mackenzie warned that anyone captured probably would be shot by Indians or Mexicans but mentioned nothing about his lack of formal authority.

The Fourth crossed in the darkness at Sycamore Ford, between Quemado and the Las Moras. Excitement masked their tiredness from the many miles covered that day. Below the river the country was "a dreary, almost waterless waste of mountains and trackless deserts" known to few North Americans. The Apache had hidden from the Spanish there; now it was sanctuary for the Kickapoo, Lipan, and Pottawottami who raided Texas ranches. The enmity of the Kickapoo was the result of their being attacked by Texans as they moved to Mexico from their reservation during the Civil War. Having traversed the canebrakes and chaparral and

Colonel Ranald Mackenzie was a brilliant cavalry commander during the Civil War. Afterward he ended the problem of Indian raids from south of the Rio Grande.

reached open ground, about 10 p.m., Mackenzie put the regiment into a trot. For maximum surprise the attack had to be made at day break. The heavily-laden mules held back the rest of the column, for the company could "only move as fast as its slowest unit, and this impeding unit was the slowest mule in that pack train." Furthermore, the supplies might be lost if hostile Indians or Mexicans got between the troopers and the mule train. Mackenzie ordered the men to stuff their pockets with hard bread; already they were carrying the reserve ammunition. The packs were cut away and the mules, Carter wrote, "freed of their burdens, trotted along like kittens the remainder of the night."

Near dawn on May 18 men and animals were near exhaustion from "the killing gait." Carter saw Van, McLain, and Cox in front of the main body "constantly plying their braided quirts, and with their heels vigorously helping their beasts along, never swerving a hair from the general direction taken the evening before." Behind the Seminole Negro scouts, in columns of four, came the regiment.

At daylight, using the cover provided by the valley of the Rio San Rodrigo, the men and horses drank, equipment was inspected, and cinches were tightened. Moving up out of the valley they saw, at the foot of a long slope, Indian huts. The three villages averaged about sixty lodges each. The largest, the Kickapoo, was the nearest; the Lipan was about a quarter of a mile away. The Fourth charged across a mile of rough ground. McLaughlin's I Troop was in front; it pursued the Indians who fled, while the other companies attacked in a column of platoons, firing a volley, moving aside to reload, and coming back to fire again as they swept alongside the towns.

The villages were fired. The lodges, of rushes or grass, with thatched rooves, and "dry as tinder, flashed up, roared and burned like powder." The troopers seized forty or fifty prisoners and about 200 horses, mostly branded stock stolen in Texas. The Indian casualties exceeded the nineteen warriors Mackenzie reported. After a seven-hour halt the Fourth commenced its retreat by a new route, through the village of Remolino and across sixty miles of rough Coahuila country, peopled by hostile Indians and Mexicans. Carter wrote:

> It was a scalding day; not a breath of air stirred . . . . Our trail had been discovered going in, and the results of our raid had been communicated by rapid runners or couriers up and down the river . . . . As darkness settled about us our anxiety increased . . . *We did not feel safe,* and we fully realized that the worst was before us, this interminable night of gloom and uncertainty.

The captured Indian women and children were hostages to be used in forcing the Kickapoo onto their reservation in the Indian Territory. "Towards morning the Indian papooses or children, in some cases mounted with the squaws by twos and threes upon the ponies, began to be troublesome by falling fast asleep and tumbling off on the trail . . . They were finally lashed on with lariats . . . ."

Again and again the Seminole warned of the presence of enemy forces, but there was no attack. Carter wrote: "It was a long, long, night. Everywhere the men drowsed and swayed in their saddles." Two troopers traveled by litter; one would die just as he entered the United States. "*Sleep* was the one relief sought for . . . woe betide any sleeper who might be caught off his guard, for the rear was being dogged by raging, cruel foes who had their homes and kindred to avenge." Men suffered from sleep deprivation; their judgment was poor and they hallucinated. By dawn the retreat had lasted fifteen hours and when they struck the Rio Grande about fifteen miles below Del Rio:

> Some of the men were fast asleep low down on their saddles with their arms tightly clasped about their horses' necks; others were drowsing and swaying or

nodding bolt upright . . . . The condition of the prisoners, although ludicrous, was pitiful in the extreme. They had been riding, lashed on the captured ponies, doubled up and by threes . . . . All faces wore that dull gray, ashy, death-like appearance indicative of overworked nature . . . .

The Fourth camped on Green Van's ranch, where Lieutenant Henry Lawton met them with supplies. For the first time in 49 hours the horses were unsaddled. Mexicans and Indians gathered across the river shouted threats. Mackenzie posted sentries while the rest of the regiment tried to sleep. Carter, who had not slept in four nights, complained, "The field proved to be an immense ant-heap. The little pests attacked, bit, persecuted and tortured us until early morning, when we moved to a more secure spot."

The Fourth left for Fort Clark on May 20. That evening Mackenzie revealed that they had invaded Mexico without a written order. Pointing out that Mackenzie had acted illegally, Captain Beaumont stated that any member of the command would have been justified in not crossing the border. Captain N. B. McLaughlin, a former Civil War general, said he would not have gone had he known the truth.

Mackenzie announced, "Any officer or man who had refused to follow me across the river I would have shot."

McLaughlin—by Carter's estimate the Army's second best marksman with pistol or carbine—replied, "That would depend, sir, upon who shot first."

A special session of the Texas legislature, on May 25, by joint resolution thanked Mackenzie's Fourth Cavalry for inflicting "punishment upon a band of Kickapoo Indians who, harbored and fostered by the Mexican authorities, have, for years past been waging a predatory warfare upon the frontier of Texas, murdering our citizens, conveying their children into captivity, and plundering their property . . . ."

The ride—159 miles in 32 marching hours—was among the longest in the history of American cavalry. Beginning at 3:30 on the morning of May 17 the troopers traveled twenty miles to the Las Moras rendezvous, then twelve miles to the Rio Grande; they left the river at about 8:30 p.m., rode 58 miles and reached the Rio San Rodrigo at 4:30 a.m. on May 18. After the attack a few hours were spent rounding up stolen stock and prisoners; leaving the Indian villages at about 1 p.m., the Fourth traveled 69 miles to Green Van's ranch, arriving there at 4 a.m. on May 19. Returning home, encumbered by prisoners and stolen horses, the regiment averaged 4.6 miles an hour.

General Sheridan stated, "There cannot be any valid boundary when we pursue Indians who murder our people and carry away our property." Maintaining that the expedition was in the interest of peace Mackenzie reminded Mexican authorities that three militia companies from Mexico attacked a Lipan camp on Texas' Pecos River and took prisoners in 1869. Mexico lodged a mild protest eight months later.

Mackenzie had stopped raids that had cost property and innocent lives; later it was clear that the Kickapoo would not have moved to the Indian Territory otherwise. The hostages were taken to San Antonio and then Fort Gibson. A number of Kickapoo joined them there; in 1875 another 114 made the move, leaving about the same number in Mexico. Felipe and Dolores La Torre wrote that Kickapoo now living in Mexico still dislike blacks because the Seminole Negroes helped Mackenzie.

Grierson Commanded The Tenth Cavalry

Benjamin Grierson, born July 8, 1826, in Pittsburgh, Pennsylvania, wanted to be a soldier, but his Irish immigrant parents insisted that he study music. (When "Swedish Nightingale" Jenny Lind gave five concerts in St. Louis, Grierson's sister reported, "Ben heard them all.") Unable to earn a living as a bandmaster and music teacher, Grierson became a merchant.

In 1861 Grierson enlisted in the Army as a private but soon became colonel of the Sixth Illinois Cavalry. Detesting horses, probably because a pony kicked him in the face when he was eight years old, Grierson was a superb cavalry officer.

His sixteen-day raid, in April, 1863, covered 600 miles of enemy country, from La Grange, Mississippi, to Baton Rouge, Louisiana, and took pressure off U. S. Grant's forces moving against Vicksburg. "General Grierson was the first officer to set the example of what might be done in the interior of the enemy's country without a base from which to draw supplies," said Grant.

By the close of the war Grierson was a major general of volunteers. He was tall and slender, possessed great stamina, a fine wit, a tendency toward profanity and a kindly disposition. In 1866, reduced to the rank of colonel, he began raising the Tenth Cavalry, a black regiment. Because of his high standards the recruiting required more than a year. Companies went to duty as soon as they were ready, for full regiments were not needed for Indian defense.

Major Anson Mills gave this estimate of Grierson:

> A big-hearted man, the only experience Grierson had in military affairs was as a general of volunteers, with which he was successful. With no experience in the regular army, even the best intentions did not fit him for the required discipline. He left the details of the post and regiment entirely to me, signing only papers which went to his superiors. He was too prone to forgive offenses and trust to promises for reform, which rendered the discipline and reputation of the regiment poor.

Grierson built Fort Sill and was the post commander in 1871 when Colonel Ranald Mackenzie arrested Satanta, Satank, and Big Tree for the killing of seven members of Henry Warren's wagon train. Parts of the Tenth Cavalry were stationed at forts Richardson, Griffin, and Concho while Grierson and the balance operated from Fort Sill in the 1874 campaigns. After Fort Concho—240 miles west of San Antonio and 500 miles east of El Paso—became Grierson's headquarters, on one reporting date six troops and the band, in which Grierson was greatly interested, were with him, two each were at forts Griffin and McKavett, one was at Fort Davis, and the other at Fort Stockton. In nineteen years the regiment's twelve troops were never in one place.

Grierson expanded Fort Concho and opened roads to connect the posts housing his regiment. According to Frank Millet, Grierson described the embryo San Angelo as two dozen hovels housing "whiskey shops or something worse" and reported:

> Now this whole section of the country is overrun with the greatest set of scoundrels that ever rode on the face of the earth and went unharmed, and constant murders are committed and robberies perpetrated. The sheriff of this

Ben Grierson, a Civil War general, disliked horses but was one of the best of the Union cavalry commanders.

county is a gambler and keeps his drinking saloon in the city aforesaid. He is as great a rascal as any, no doubt, but altogether they have lively times and frequent arrests are made, and as their city is not provided with a jail those rascals have to be confined in the guardhouse. I have notified the civil authorities that they must find some other place for their unwanted rascals . . . .

Fort Concho was equally unimpressive:

In all my Army experience I have never been closer to anything that is conducted in such a haphazard . . . and disjointed manner . . . . The records are in very bad condition and there is no plan here of the post or the buildings. All is out of repair and there seems never to have been any determined effort on the part of anyone to go to the trouble to secure the authority or materials for needed repairs . . . . There is not a nail or board at the post to have even a coffin made for a soldier in case of death . . . .

Grierson was dismayed by the abundance of dogs. The holes they dug pocked Fort Concho's parade ground; once Grierson on "not a good morning for dogs" counted 51 vagrant hounds. Old soldier H. H. McConnell, recalling his Sixth Cavalry service at Fort Richardson about that time, wrote:

Our regiment was always overrun with dogs—"Mongrel, puppy, whelp, and hound, and curs of low degree,"—some valuable greyhounds among them, but mostly of the "yaller dog" species. At the sound of the bugle every dog would set up a bawl, until at times the nuisance would become epidemic, as it were, and a special order be issued to exterminate all those running loose on the parade ground. Our company had a big, hairy, nondescript dog that "joined" at Jacksboro in 1868 . . . . He tramped along with the guard to Kansas when the regiment was moved there in 1871, and I last saw him at Fort Hays in the fall of that year, growing old "in the service."

Grierson's men built the telegraph line from Fort Davis to El Paso. They escorted trail drives, stage coaches and railroad surveyors and spent months pursuing the Mimbres Apache Victorio in Texas and New Mexico. (Mexican troops finally killed Victorio in October, 1880.)

From Fort Davis, in 1885 Grierson took the regiment—the first time it had ever been together—to Arizona for the campaign against the Apache of Geronimo and Cochise. He left the Tenth Cavalry after twenty-two years to succeed General George Crook as commander of the Department of Arizona. Officers of his regiment gave him a Tiffany-made saber; one side of the blade was engraved with the states and territories in which the Tenth had campaigned: Kansas, Oklahoma, Colorado, Texas, New Mexico and Arizona. The opposite side bore a remark made by U. S. Grant after Vicksburg: "I need more cavalry and a Grierson to command them." After retiring as a brigadier general in 1890, Grierson ranched near Fort Davis. His first wife, Alice Kirk, died in 1888, and he married Lillian Atwood King in 1897. Grierson died at his summer home in Owena, Michigan, on September 1, 1911.

Grierson, as commander, renovated and expanded Fort Concho.

In his last years of service in Texas with the Tenth Cavalry, Grierson operated from Fort Davis.

Fort Davis was headquarters for Benjamin Grierson's Tenth Cavalry, which was scattered over Texas.

Uncle Charlie Carlton Ran A College

Charles Carlton, born in Kent County, England, ran away to sea at the age of sixteen. He studied under Alexander Campbell at Bethany College, graduating in 1849. The turmoil attending the slave controversy and secession disrupted his teaching in Springfield, Missouri, and Carlton relocated in Texas for the duration of the war. He organized the Dallas congregation that became the Central Christian Church. Carlton was returning to Missouri when he stopped in Grayson County. As Randolph Clark, a founder—with his brother Addison—of Texas Christian University, told it:

At the close of the war, while waiting for peace to be restored in Missouri, he secured a building in the village of Kentuckytown and began teaching. The school was crowded from the first day. Many had been deprived of the opportunities of going to school through the years of war, and lost no time in taking advantage of this privilege. After the second year, he decided to remain in Texas. The citizens of Bonham offered him a suitable building and equipment and he moved and settled permanently in their midst.

Nothing resembling Carlton's school existed later, Clark stated.

The teacher was the school; students came from far and near, many of them boys in years, who had developed into men by the hardships of war. The school was to them the opportunity for making up for the four years which had been cut out of their lives when they would have been getting an education.

In the school's program, there was not time for idling . . . . Each student selected the studies he especially needed, finished them and pushed on to others. While the teacher held some in classes, others would be scattered in groups, under trees or in the sunshine, all intent on some task and needing the teacher only when they met some obstacle in the path of progress. Mr. Carlton's personal presence and his daily life before the students were a source of inspiration.

The Clarks were among those inspired. After Confederate service, in late 1866 they entered the Kentuckytown school. In January of 1869, after completing his Carlton College studies, Addison Clark married Sallie McQuigg, Mrs. Carlton's niece.

Carlton moved to Bonham in 1868; as Carlton College his school functioned for 34 years, educating thousands of valuable citizens. Its three departments, primary, preparatory and collegiate, were housed on the campus of the defunct female academy. Carlton organized Bonham's First Christian Church and was its pastor until his death.

One student, Dean T. U. Taylor, of the University of Texas, left a memorable account of Carlton College.

Since the news of Uncle Charlie Carlton's school methods and training methods had spread all over North Texas . . . . I followed his advice and entered Carlton Seminary in the fall of 1877, and there I met one of those rare and radiant characters who used money as axle grease and was ever building character in the minds of the pupils, boys and girls . . . . Charles Carlton was a young boy in the shipyards of Boston working as a day laborer. One day he spelled out in the newspaper the word "algebra." He told me that at the time he did not know whether it was a snake or an elephant, but he asked his boss what the word spelled and the boss replied, "You ought to go to Alexander Campbell."

The Reverend Charles Carlton, a Disciples of Christ minister, ran Carlton College at Bonham. His students, Addison and Randolph Clark, founded Add-Ran Christian College, which became Texas Christian University.

Taylor wrote: "No poor boy ever went to Charlie Carlton, broke and helpless, and was turned away from his door . . . . Charlie Carlton was Alexander Campbell and Mark Hopkins combined. As a teacher he had few equals and no superior." Daily Charles Carlton taught from 8 a.m. to 6 p.m. and each weekend, after teaching Sunday School for two hours, he preached a sermon in the Bonham church. Classes met in a huge upstairs room, with President Carlton seated on the rostrum at one end. Students moved to the bench in front of him when it was their time to recite.

> He never taught two classes the same way and never let a student, however old, get out of English grammar. He would ask a special student if he understood a special problem. If the student said, "Yes," then came back the demand, "Stand up and tell us what you understand" . . . . Woe be unto the boy or girl who would tell him that he "understood" it and then failed on the job of explaining it.
> He ruled that school with a rod of love. In two years I never saw him whip a boy, but I have seen many boys beg him to whip them.

Carlton had a unique method of punishment. After summoning the offender to the dais, he would seat the boy on his knee and ask if the student wanted his parents informed about his misbehavior. Everyone would be watching, and the culprit would be weeping by then. Announcing that it was his duty to punish the offender severely, Carlton would kiss him on each cheek. The students would collapse laughing while the embarrassed boy returned to his seat aware that news of the event would precede him all over Fannin County.

At first Carlton College was co-educational. The 1887 enrollment of 240 included 103 boys, but it became a school for girls the next year.

Taylor wrote of Carlton's influence on the Clarks at Thorp Spring:

> It all grew out of the mind and inspiration of Uncle Charlie Carlton in Bonham, Texas. Addran College was later moved to Waco and its name was changed to Texas Christian University. Still later it was moved to Fort Worth . . . . There on its walls hangs a picture of Uncle Charlie Carlton when he moulded the minds and souls and character of Addison and Randolph Clark.

Carlton College, a family enterprise, suffered when Mrs. Carlton died in 1900. After the death of Professor Carlton, on February 13, 1902, his son, Charles T. Carlton, became president. In 1910 the three-story frame building which served for offices, classrooms and dormitory burned. It was not insured. In 1914 a merger was attempted with Sherman's Carr-Burdette College; Charles T. Carlton was president of the new school, but problems aggravated by the war caused the arrangement to fail.

Kenneth Hay, in his fine thesis about Carlton, quoted the following introductory statement from a pageant presented at Bonham:

> We . . . feel that the outstanding event of importance to this town was the coming of "Uncle Charley Carlton" to establish the school and later organize a congregation and form a church here. Bonham, then a small village, grew up around Carlton College.

Near the close of his life Charles Carlton once was asked, "When you began this school did you feel that it would turn out to be a financial success?" The old man answered "I never even thought of that side of it."

T. U. Taylor, third from left, a graduate of Carlton College, was for decades a dean of the University of Texas. Fifth from left is United States Senator Morris Sheppard and Dr. H. Y. Benedict, president of the University of Texas, is on the right.

"80 John" Wallace Was A Rancher

Born into slavery, Daniel Webster "80 John" Wallace became an influential rancher; at his death he had resided in Mitchell County longer than anyone else. He was the son of Mary Wallace, of Virginia, whose first three children were born in Missouri; Mary O'Daniel, of Victoria County, had paid $1,000 for her. Hetty Wallace Branch wrote of her grandmother, Mary Wallace:

> Mary's attractiveness was mostly in the way she held her head in walking, and in the neatness and the coil of long black hair at the nape of her neck . . . . Mrs. O'Daniel was very pleased and permitted Mary to bring her son to the "Big House" where she could attend him while working. Mrs. O'Daniel's son and Webster were almost the same age. Mary nursed the two boys and fed them often from the milk of her breast.

Wallace, born in Victoria County on September 15, 1860, worked as a field hand for 50¢ a day, but his ambition was to be a cowhand. He was only a boy when he made his first trail drive, to Coleman County; his pay was $15. Wallace worked for Indian fighter Sam Gholson at Buffalo Gap, Taylor County, then hired on with John Nunn. Standing 6 feet 3 inches tall at the age of seventeen, he helped the NUN outfit drive the first herd into Scurry County. Nunn's headquarters were located about ten miles east of Hide Town (present Snyder).

On December 12, 1878, Wallace went to work for Clay Mann, who was moving South Texas cattle—some of the first stock grazed in Mitchell County—onto his range near present Colorado City. It was then that Wallace acquired the nickname "80 John," for Mann's brand was a huge 80 extending from backbone to belly.

Mann ran cattle in three Texas counties, three New Mexico counties, and the Mexican state of Chihuahua. During the terrible 1883 drought Mann's brother, John, and some other hands, including Wallace, drove part of the stock to the ranch in Mexico; there an Indian shot John Mann through the head with an arrow. Clay Mann ordered the herd driven back to the United States and sold the Chihuahua ranch to Senator George Hearst, of California, the father of William Randolph Hearst.

While employed by Mann, Wallace received a letter stating that his mother was quite ill. She had moved to Fayette County with the O'Daniels; they were, her granddaughter recalled, "the warmest of friends. After Emancipation Mary, the slave, continued to love and serve Mary, the mistress. After the death of Mary Wallace, Mary O'Daniel took her two youngest sons to raise." The letter reached Wallace a month after it was mailed, and by the time he got to Fayette County, his mother was dead. Wallace returned to West Texas.

Mann set much store by his employee's judgment. When someone offered to wager on the number of cattle in a herd he agreed on condition that he could first consult Wallace, who estimated the herd to be not quite 5,000. The tally then showed the exact number to be 4,975 cattle. Once Wallace took $30,000 to Midland—a three-day journey—for his employer. For two years Mann retained part of Wallace's pay, and with $600 saved in that fashion Wallace bought his first cattle, which he branded and turned in with Mann's herd. In 1885 Wallace acquired two sections of land southeast of Loraine, Mitchell County.

118

"80 John" Wallace got his nickname while working for Clay Mann, whose brand was a huge 80. He was a very successful rancher near Loraine and had lived in Mitchell County longer than anyone else at the time of his death.

Conscious of his lack of education—about three months of school—at 25 Wallace rode east and entered the second grade of a school for blacks in Navarro County. That winter and the next he studied, while working his ranch in the other seasons. He and a friend bought twelve acres of land, intending to raise cotton, but one day his plow got stuck and he stalked away and did not return for twenty years.

In Navarro County Wallace married Laura Deloach Owen, who was finishing high school and had planned to teach. They moved into a house on one of the Mann ranches. After Clay Mann's death in 1889 Wallace worked for his widow and trained his sons as cowmen.

After fourteen years Wallace devoted full time to his own business, although sometimes he had to work for others to make ends meet. An early member of the Texas and Southwestern Cattle Raisers Association, he attended its meetings for thirty years. Dry spells were frequent and his losses were heavy, but he persevered. He drilled water wells, acquired more land, and put 1,200 acres into cotton and feed. Ten tenant families lived on his ranch.

In the middle of the depression Wallace had twelve and a half sections of land and 600 Hereford cattle and no debts. The ranch, still intact, is owned by his family. He helped others and gave to worthy causes. The D. W. Wallace School, in Colorado City, is named for him. He died on March 28, 1939, and was buried on the first section he ever owned.

Hetty Branch, recalling her father's last days, wrote that "80 John" Wallace said to his wife, "I am going to leave you."

She replied, "You must not. How can I live without you?"

"It is just as natural to die as to live. Do the best you can. Sing 'On Jordan's Stormy Banks I Stand.'"

Later Wallace stated, "I have reviewed my life from six years on until now. I have harmed no man. I am ready to go. What do you think of me?"

Mrs. Wallace bent and kissed him. She said, "You have always been my ideal, don't you know?"

A few years earlier John Hendrix wrote:

> He is held in high esteem by the citizens of Mitchell County. At each meeting of an organization of pioneers of the section, he is called on to say a few words, and in a manner deferential and in language wholly lacking in Uncle Remus dialect, he tells them of their country as he first saw it more than half a century ago, unsullied by barbed wire and train smoke, a cowman's paradise of running water, grass-covered hills and wide fertile valleys, where antelope played, and the South Texas cows of Mr. Clay Mann grazed among the still fresh carcasses of the slaughtered buffaloes.

Laura DeLoach Owen married Daniel Webster Wallace and helped build the Mitchell County ranch which is still owned by her children and grandchildren.

T. V. Munson Received the French Legion of Honor

Thomas Volney Munson, born in Illinois on September 26, 1843, taught school after graduating from business college, then earned a bachelor's degree from Kentucky State Agricultural College. Munson submitted his thesis on "Trees and Forests of Texas" and his master's degree was conferred by his alma mater—now the University of Kentucky—in 1873. Visiting the Lexington vineyard of his former professor, Robert Peters, Munson became interested in grapes. Peters gave him seeds for 30 to 40 varieties; Munson planted them at his Lincoln, Nebraska, home but was not successful in raising grapes there.

In April of 1876 Munson opened a nursery business at Denison, which had been founded four years earlier by his younger brother, William B. Munson. After exploring timbered areas on Red River where grapes grew in abundance, T. V. Munson announced:

> Here were six or eight good species of wild grapes, several of which had not been seen by me previously. I had found my grape paradise! Surely now, thought I, "this is the place for experimentation with grapes!"

(The Canadian St. Denis had been equally enthusiastic over grapes grown by Tejas Indians 200 miles southeast of Grayson County. Carlos Castañeda quoted a letter of St. Denis written about 1715: "Their lands are all cultivated and there is no fruit in the world richer than that found here, nor more wonderful grapes of various kinds and colors in such quantities. The bunches are as large as twenty-eight and thirty-pound shot.")

With renewed interest Munson decided to make a comprehensive study of grapes, to familiarize himself with every species and learn the appropriate climate and soil for each. Later he recalled:

> At various times during the past thirty years the writer travelled through forty of the states and territories of the Union, never neglecting any opportunity to hunt and study the wild plants, especially the grapes and other fruits. In these journeys, not less than 50,000 miles were travelled by railway and many hundreds on horseback and on foot, and thousands of vines of nearly every species of American grape were studied, growing in their native habitats.

Munson experimented with vines, and having found many errors in earlier classifications, he introduced a more thorough and natural system. His articles on new species he had discovered appeared in leading journals and his correspondents included French expert Pierre Viala, for whom Munson named his daughter, Viala.

At the 1885 New Orleans Cotton Centennial, Munson exhibited specimens of every kind of American grape. Similar collections were presented to Harvard, Columbia, Cornell and eleven agricultural colleges. At Chicago's Columbian Exposition, in 1893, Munson showed all American species and most Asian varieties in "the most complete botanical display of the grape genus ever made." That exhibit was donated to the United States Department of Agriculture, which had published his *Classification and Generic Synopsis of the Wild Grapes of North America* in 1890.

122

Thomas Volney Munson settled in Denison soon after it was founded by his brother, W. B. Munson.

Munson experimented with hybrids in an attempt to perfect the grape, which he considered "the most beautiful, most wholesome and nutritious, most certain and profitable fruit that can be grown." He hoped to combine the best wild and cultivated strains to produce new varieties with the finest qualities. (Munson believed the market demanded three colors: bright red, black or dark purple, and yellow; grapes which were green when ripe did not sell well.) His book, *Foundations of American Grape Culture*, was the outstanding work on the subject.

When French vineyards were attacked by phylloxera, an insect which causes roots to enlarge and die, the damage was so extensive as to jeopardize the nation's economy. The French government sent representatives to solicit Munson's advice. There was no practical way to destroy the pests; the only workable solution was to graft susceptible varieties onto resistant stocks. Munson suggested a type that could withstand the attack of the plant louse and shipped a boatload of mustang grape stalks to France.

Through use of the Texas plants the French wine industry was saved; in 1888 the French Minister of Agriculture, Pierre Viala, came to Denison and conferred upon Munson the title of Chevalier du Merit Agricole. Munson was the second American—after Thomas Alva Edison—to receive the French Legion of Honor. Much wine made in France now comes from vines with Texas origins. (While most sources claim that the vines sent to France were from Grayson County, the *Encyclopedia of Texas* states that two Bell County species furnished the stocks upon which the French vines were grafted.)

Munson's university made him an honorary doctor of science and he was a member of the American Academy of Science when he died in 1913. When the Munson nurseries were sold, in 1938, many varieties of his grapes had been lost, but recent efforts have been made to locate them. The T. V. Munson Memorial Vineyard was established in 1975 at Grayson County College, and more than 115 varieties have been found and planted there.

T. V. Munson established a nursery business in Denison and experimented with grapes.

The home of T. V. Munson, formerly located outside of Denison, is now surrounded by residential development.

Munson became one of the world's authorities on grapes while discovering many new varieties in Texas. When French vineyards were destroyed by phylloxera, Munson proposed the use of stocks from Texas, which saved the wine industry of France and earned for Munson the French Legion of Honor.

Gorgas Began His Crusade Against Yellow Fever at Fort Brown

William Crawford Gorgas, whose father, General Josiah Gorgas, had been the Confederate chief of ordnance, hoped for a military career. After graduating from the University of the South, where his father was vice-chancellor, Gorgas tried without success to get into West Point. Resolving to join the Army as a physician, Gorgas entered Bellevue Medical College, in New York City. Under the influence of Dr. William Welch, medicine became more than a means to obtain a commission. Gorgas graduated in 1879. Upon completing his internship at Bellevue he joined the Army despite the protests of his father, the president of the University of Alabama.

After serving at forts Clark and Duncan, in August of 1882 Gorgas was sent to Fort Brown; yellow fever had broken out in Brownsville and 2,300 cases had been reported. Gorgas had never seen a yellow fever patient. The post commander was Colonel William Lyster, whose sister-in-law Gorgas married; the first time Marie Doughty ever saw Gorgas was while riding at Fort Brown.

> Nearby lay the historic battlefields of Palo Alto and Resaca de la Palma, the favourite destination of our rides in normal times. On that particular day our ride was limited to the post, because we were quarantined against the neighbouring town of Brownsville on account of the yellow fever epidemic then raging.

She was stricken a few days later and Gorgas was her physician. She wrote:

> Yellow fever is not a lingering illness. The patient is usually convalescent or dead within a week of the time he is stricken. On the fourth or fifth day of my sickness I was apparently in the last stages of the disease . . . . all hopes of my recovery had been abandoned.

Fort Brown's cemetery was on an island in the lagoon. To avoid delay in burial, an open grave was kept ready for the fever's next victim. Fear of the disease caused the physicians to be undertaker, grave-digger, and minister, conducting the funeral while the family remained at a distance. Gorgas had promised to read Miss Doughty's burial service and her grave was ready when she began to recover. Then Gorgas was stricken; she declared that "yellow fever made its first and last attack on its mortal enemy." The courtship began as they were convalescing. She moved to Fort Clark with the Lysters while Gorgas spent the next two years at Fort Brown. They married in 1885.

Because of his immunity the Army sent Gorgas to work where epidemics were in progress. He had charge of the yellow fever camp at Siboney, Cuba, during the Spanish-American War. Believing the illness came from lack of sanitation Gorgas advised burning Siboney to destroy fever-causing germs. The village and all medical and quartermaster supplies were put to the torch.

In December of 1898 Gorgas, as chief sanitary officer, was sent to Havana, where yellow fever had existed for 150 years. If Havana could be eliminated as a focus of infection Gorgas believed the United States would be free of yellow fever. He assumed the disease was

William Gorgas, as a young physician at Fort Brown, caught yellow fever. Because of his acquired immunity he was sent to work in other yellow fever epidemics.

transmitted by contact with a patient. There were then few cases in Havana; only later did he realize that the low incidence was due to withdrawal of the soldiers and absence of visitors, who were the only potential victims. The natives, having been exposed, were immune. Gorgas wrote:

> Had Athens been subject to yellow fever in the time of Alcibiades, yellow fever would certainly be there today. All the citizens of the city of Athens would have become immune, but a sufficient number of Greeks would have been constantly coming into the city from the interior to have kept the disease endemic, exactly as has occurred in our time at Havana.

In 1899 many Spaniards moved to Havana and the fever broke out again, Gorgas renewed his campaign to clean up the filthy streets, which held everything from dead horses to human bodies. The general health improved and smallpox diminished, but yellow fever increased. Gorgas observed: "When we went to Havana we knew no more of the sanitation of yellow fever than we knew a century before." In 1900 about 25,000 immigrants, mostly Spanish, arrived, fueling the epidemic in spite of Havana's new cleanliness. The cause was not poor sanitation.

For a generation Dr. Carlos Finlay had taught that the Stegomyia mosquito, one of hundreds of varieties, carried yellow fever. Unfortunately his experiments disproved the theory, for the laboratory mosquitos did not transfer the disease. Gorgas recalled "having spent a good many hours trying to show Dr. Finlay the absurdity of his mosquito theory of the transmission of yellow fever, but the doctor was a veteran who already had sixteen years experience in meeting arguments of other men like myself." Finlay was encouraged by recent evidence of insect carriers. In 1889 two physicians proved that the Texas fever, which afflicted cattle, was transmitted by a tick, and Ronald Ross, in 1897, discovered that the Anopheles mosquito carried malaria.

As the epidemic worsened, in 1900 a commission of four medical officers was sent to Cuba. Dr. Walter Reed, a Virginian who had studied under Dr. William Welch at Johns Hopkins University, and his colleagues worked with Gorgas. Fortunately they had Dr. Henry Carter's results, demonstrating that yellow fever had a ten-to fourteen-day incubation period. Reed suspected involvement of an insect host. In fact, Finlay's theory was sound. His twenty years of experiments failed to support him because he did not know that (1) in order to become infected the mosquito had to bite a yellow fever patient during the first three days of illness, and that (2) the mosquito could not pass the disease for ten to fourteen days. While Reed's board was understanding this "extrinsic incubation" one commissioner died and another got sick after being bitten by infected mosquitos.

At first Gorgas was skeptical, believing Reed might have discovered one of several causes. After accepting Reed's conclusions Gorgas despaired, for destruction of the mosquitos seemed impossible. Consideration was given to immunization by innoculation, but the death of Clara Maas and another volunteer indicated that vaccination was too hazardous. The solution was destruction of the Stegomyia mosquito, which lived around towns because of their taste for human blood. Disdaining natural collections of water they laid their eggs in still, clear water held by man-made containers near human habitations. The mosquito attacked the ankle or the underside of the wrist where the skin was tender and chances of being killed were slight. Only the females bit; human blood was not ingested for sustenance but because of some biological need existing prior to laying eggs.

Gorgas had receptacles emptied and water barrels screened. Kerosene was poured on standing bodies of water to kill larvae and young mosquitoes. The results were dramatic.

130

Gorgas became Surgeon General of the United States. He was decorated by the British king for his efforts against malaria and yellow fever.

Havana had not experienced a fever-free day since 1762, and in the last decade of the 19th century hundreds died annually; 1,282 died of yellow fever in 1896 and 310 in 1900. Gorgas began battling the Stegomyia in March of 1901. The fever claimed only five lives in the next four years. An outbreak in 1905 was quickly checked, and for eighteen years Havana did not experience a single case of yellow fever.

Reed, who died in 1902, and Gorgas maintained the highest regard for each other. To one alluding to his greatness, Gorgas responded that he had merely followed "in the footsteps of a great man—Walter Reed."

Gorgas conquered the yellow fever epidemic that had hampered construction of the Panama Canal. The French had lost 250 of every 1,000 employees when they attempted such a project. Gorgas then became interested in malaria. In 1914, the year of the canal's opening, the death rate of the Canal Zone was six per thousand compared to fourteen per thousand in the United States.

Major General Gorgas was offered, and declined, the presidencies of the University of the South and the University of Alabama. As Surgeon-General of the United States he retired three days after the Armistice. He suffered a stroke while in England. King George V came to his hospital room to confer the rank of Knight Commander of the Order of St. Michael and St. George. Gorgas died in London on July 3, 1920, and was given a British Major General's funeral in St. Paul's Cathedral; he was buried in Arlington National Cemetery.

The work of William C. Gorgas in wiping out yellow fever began at the Fort Brown hospital which is now used by Texas Southmost College.

Bloys Held a Camp Meeting for Cowboys

In October of 1890 the Reverend William T. Bloys, a Presbyterian minister, and a congregation made up of pioneers and cowhands held their first meeting at Skillman's Grove, sixteen miles southwest of Fort Davis. The Cowboy Camp Meeting, convened every year since then, has made substantial contributions to life in the Big Bend country.

At the first gathering, held in the shade of a great live oak tree, were Baptists, Methodists, Disciples of Christ and Presbyterians, but sessions have always been open to everyone. An Arbuckle's Coffee box served as Bloys' pulpit for the weekend meeting. The people came by wagon and horseback. Minnie Clifton wrote:

They camped together, the women and children sleeping in the wagons, and the men in bed rolls or blankets on the ground. Camp fires, old fashioned Dutch ovens, and skillets furnished the cooking facilities, the women in sunbonnets and cook aprons bending to their tasks.

The 46 individuals attending that first year included the families of George Evans, John Zack Means, Bill Jones, Ote Finley, and Bill Kingston.

The grove of live oaks chosen as the meeting place was named for Henry Skillman, in 1850 the first contractor providing monthly mail service between San Antonio and present El Paso. Originally owned by Simeon Hart, a founder of El Paso, the beautiful site in the Davis Mountains foothills was the campground of Skillman and his employee, Big Foot Wallace.

In the *Christian Science Monitor* for July 26, 1921, Barry Scobee wrote:

Cowboys worth hundreds of thousands of dollars and cowboys worth only their horse and saddle in material goods eat from the same pot and sit side by side to hear the preaching and have an equal voice in the conduct of the association .... The cattlemen are great hosts. The tribal days of Judea are suggested by the way the families stick together in family tribes. Sons and daughters, grandchildren and great-grandchildren gather in tents and cottages around a great central oak tree. Every tribe has an oak tree, some three or four. Some of the camps entertain hundreds of visitors; no stranger may go to the meeting and remain unprovided for.

The Trans-Pecos country was late in settlement. The state's last Indian troubles occurred there, and the railroad arrived in 1882, about the same time as the cattlemen. The Reverend William B. Bloys, born in Tennessee in 1847, had moved to Fort Davis in an effort to recover his health. Bloys weighed about 120 pounds, had black hair and a drooping moustache. He worked his way through Lane Theological Seminary in Cincinnatti, Ohio, and was 32 years old at graduation. His physical condition kept Bloys from working in foreign missions, as he had wished; instead the Presbyterian Church, U.S.A. assigned him to Coleman, Texas. Within a decade Bloys organized churches in such towns as Ballinger, Paint Rock, Buffalo Gap, and Coleman. An attack of measles so weakened him that a physician advised another move about the time friends asked that he come to Jeff Davis County. Bloys, his wife, and four children arrived in Fort Davis in February of 1888.

As he traveled the sparsely-populated country, visiting and preaching in the isolated homes, Bloys baptized settlers into whatever church was requested. One day Mrs. John

The Reverend William B. Bloys founded the Cowboy Camp Meeting at Skillman's Grove in the Davis Mountains.

Means stated that there should be a place for cowboys and ranch people to meet for worship, and Bloys converted the idea into reality. The first meeting led to Bloys holding regular services at Marfa and Alpine and so stimulated the growth of his Fort Davis congregation as to require a larger church. Bloys carved the pulpit and did much of the construction himself.

Attendance at the Cowboy Camp Meeting grew from year to year. Joe Evans recalled that meals were built around an antelope entree; his father and a friend killed nine on the way to Skillman's Grove one year. Dining halls were built on the grounds, and cooks were employed. A big tent sheltered the congregation after the tree was outgrown; then a sheet iron tabernacle was erected to seat 1,000, the number attending in 1913.

For $1,280 John Means bought the section where Skillman's Grove stood and in 1900 conveyed it to the Bloys Camp Meeting Association. The tabernacle was enlarged in 1939, and chairs were substituted for some of the benches. Reading rooms were built, and individuals placed cabins on sites made available by the association, which also provided free wood, water and electricity. The present caretaker's home was originally built for storage. Until 1920 lanterns and gas lights were used. Bloys always consulted an almanac in choosing the meeting date so that a full moon helped with the lighting problem. (There is, or was, a light plant on the grounds.)

Other preachers shared the pulpit with Bloys. Ministers from each of the four founding denominations were present, and traditionally there were four preaching services daily. The Baptist G. W. Truett and Presbyterian John Burma, president of Trinity University, were among the visiting preachers. Bloys was precise about arrangements. Evans wrote that when dogs "jumped a wild cat up on the side of the mountain" and chased it through camp:

> they turned over the coffee pot, threw gravel in the frijole beans and gravy, then run right by the corner of the brush arbor where Brother Bloys was praying. All of us boys jumped up and took after the dogs. They treed the wild cat. Some of the boys had a pistol so we killed the wild cat . . . . At the next service he made this announcement, "There will be no more dogs on the camp ground."

None have been allowed since.

Evans told of the Reverend L. R. Millican, who baptised the Baptists. Once as several converts stood in the old water hole and Millican was beginning his task, a blind man lost his guide and was wandering about lost.

> His name was Blind Meriman, a piano tuner and a fine gentleman . . . . There was an old dug well about six feet deep near the edge of the water and before we knew it Blind Meriman fell in. It didn't hurt him as the dirt was soft, but it was hard on a bunch of boys to keep a straight face. Just about the time we recovered from this, an old long-eared burro let out a bray you could hear for a mile and another one off in the pasture answered him. Old Bro. Millican couldn't hear any too well and he didn't know all this was happening.

No collection has ever been taken during a service and nothing has ever been sold on the grounds. Donations are accepted but never sought, and expenses are paid by the association, with members at annual business meetings simply dividing the sum among themselves.

Bloys continued missionary work for the rest of his life, near the end driving a Model T someone had given him. (Not until about 1910 was there a car at Skillman's Grove.) He died on March 22, 1917 after managing the meeting for 27 years. Mrs. Bloys lived until 1935. At one meeting, according to the Alpine *Avalanche* obituary quoted by Minnie Clifton:

> . . . he pleaded in a feeble voice that he was growing old and a younger and stronger man should be elected to carry on the work . . . when his meaning dawned on them, members of the association in one voice cried him down. "Sit

Bloys built the Presbyterian Church in Fort Davis.

down, Bloys, there'll be time to elect your successor when you're gone," was the cry.

A monument to Bloys was dedicated at Skillman's Grove where John and Exa Means are buried. Present on the 50th anniversary were 21 who attended the first meeting. In addition to the cabins built on the grounds, during the week-long August meeting hundreds of tents shelter the 2,000 to 3,000 who attend. Many third and fourth generation descendants of the founders come from all over the nation. The Bloys meeting has inspired similar institutions in New Mexico, Wyoming, Nebraska and elsewhere in the West.

The meeting at Skillman's Grove begun by William Bloys has convened each August since the founding in 1890.

This monument was raised to the memory of the founder on the grounds of the Bloys Camp Meeting at Skillman's Grove.

140

The families who participate in the Cowboy Camp Meetings build sheet iron cabins on plots assigned to them at the grounds owned by the Bloys Association at Skillman's Grove.

The Rope-Walker Died on a Corsicana Street

Near the close of the last century a one-legged tight-wire walker contracted to perform his act in downtown Corsicana. As a promotion designed to bring people to town, he would walk a rope stretched between the tops of two business buildings across the main thoroughfare, Beaton Street. Whether it was his idea or that of the merchants, the peg-legged man—his wooden leg had a groove to accomodate the rope—carried a cast iron stove strapped on his back.

On July 28, 1898, downtown Corsicana was crowded with spectators. As the 69-year-old man—he claimed to have been born in Princeton, New Jersey on February 6, 1829—eased his way out over the street, the stove's weight made the rope sag more than he had anticipated. Halfway across Beaton Street he fell.

Mortally injured, the rope-walker called for a rabbi. There was none in Corsicana, but a Jewish merchant prayed with him in Hebrew. The dying man stated his date and place of birth, but if he gave his name, no one remembered it, and other efforts to identify him failed. Above the grave in Corsicana's Hebrew Cemetery his tombstone is inscribed "Rope Walker."

The rope walker was a performer who died after a fall from a wire over a Corsicana street.

A Wagon Train Perished in the Monahans Sand Hills

On the east side of the Pecos River a desert of sand ranging in color from light grey to yellow to reddish brown extends for more than a hundred miles. Deposited by the wind over thousands of years, some of the dunes are seventy feet high. Many, held by vegetation, are relatively stable, but most of the area is covered by migrating dunes that change shape, size, and location in response to the wind. The first Spaniards to pass through the vast desert were surprised to find the good water, acorns, and mesquite beans that made the sand hills a favorite place of white-tailed deer and other game. In earlier times mastodons and mammoths lived there, perhaps for the same reasons; shifting sands regularly expose the bones of extinct beasts and points and pottery fashioned by early man.

Three centuries after the Spanish visit Captain Randolph Marcy arrived at the Pecos River in present Ward County. Marcy's journal entry for September 24, 1849, reflects that no wagon crossing existed for forty miles to the south, a testimony to the good judgment of his guide and the Indians whose use had created the road he travelled.

> The whole surface of the country in that direction seemed to be one continuous succession of white sand hills, from twenty to one hundred feet high, in which his horses sank to their knees at almost every step, from which I infer that the route indicated by our guide is the only one in the vicinity where this formidable obstacle can be passed.

Entering the sand hills on the following day, Marcy reported:

> There is a great abundance of good water at several places in the sand hills, but it is necessary to drive animals to it, as it is half a mile from the road and wagons cannot pass near it . . . . In following up the trail from our road into the midst of this ocean of sand, we suddenly came upon several large, deep pools of pure water—the very last place on earth where one would ever think of looking for it. We are told by our guide that water can always be found here in the dry season, and, judging from the rushes and other water plants growing in the ponds, I have no doubt that is the case.

The distance across the sand hills was seventeen miles, but only about half was difficult to travel and the worst parts were as good as portions of the road along the Rio Grande. Marcy was mapping a route for the gold seekers, many of whom passed through the sand hills on the way to California.

The fate of one party which died in the sand was not known for nearly thirty years. In 1901 two cowhands, Arthur Hayes and Bob Brown, returning home from a trail drive stopped to eat at a sand hills water hole called Willow Springs, just below Flag Point. As Brown was building a fire Hayes noticed some curious objects in the sand. Knowing that the shifting sands regularly disclosed relics of the past, recent and ancient, he investigated and found the remains of a burned wagon. Before Hayes and Brown stopped digging they had discovered 39 others. The wagons had been parked in the shape of a V, with twenty on each side. Hayes wrote:

The Monahans Sand Hills stretch along the Pecos River for 100 miles. An impediment to travel in the early days, they were a good source of water for Indians and travelers.

It was apparent that the emigrants didn't expect the Indians to be hostile, because they camped in an open V, a friendly way instead of a circle form, which is the way to camp expecting any trouble. They knew the peak was the permanent camp of the Comanche tribe; it was their stronghold in the white desert sands. The peak gets its name, Flag Point, from being used as a signal point by the Indians.

Each wagon was drawn by six oxen. Hayes and Brown uncovered ox yokes, pots and pans, mining tools, scissors, knives, flintlocks, a spool bedstead, miners lamps, jewelry, a pistol, and a human yoke such as might be used on slaves.

Ward County old timers believed the wagon train was California-bound, for there were old stories of two parties of 49ers lost in the sand, but Hayes contended that it was returning from California, for westbound parties carried tools made in Philadelphia and those he found were of a kind made in San Francisco. Probably on their westward trek the travelers had found the Indians to be friendly, and did not expect trouble; "one could hire an Indian Scout to work all day long as a guide by offering him a red bandana kerchief."

Later investigation by Hayes revealed that in 1873 or 1874, while Comanche war parties were active, an eastbound wagon train with from 300 to 500 members passed through Fort Yuma, Arizona, and was never heard from again. Hayes believed that was the party which perished in the sand hills. The victims' identities were never established, for only bone fragments remained of the bodies when the wagon train was found.

Born in Llano County in 1878, Hayes was a lawman and justice of the peace. He jailed Jim Miller at Barstow, Ward County, a few months before Miller was lynched at Ada, Oklahoma. For years Hayes operated a Monahans museum exhibiting relics of the doomed wagon train and other items of historic interest. Some of his collection is owned by the Museum of the Big Bend at Sul Ross State University.

Arthur Hayes and a friend found the remains of a wagon train that had been attacked by Indians in the sand hills. Remains of 40 wagons were found at the site.

"The Eyes of Texas" Was Written for a Minstrel Show

At the close of the Civil War, Confederate general Robert E. Lee accepted the presidency of a Lexington, Virginia, college which became Washington and Lee University after his death. Lee made a profound impression upon his students, for he was finally, as Stephen Vincent Benet put it, "the prop and pillar" of the Confederacy. "The man was loved, the man was idolized, The man had every just and noble gift, He took great burdens and he bore them well."

At Washington College Lee taught that the South's recovery depended upon the efforts of the young; therefore, it was important that coming generations be well-educated. To remind students of their responsibilities, Lee customarily closed his addresses with: "Young gentlemen, remember that the eyes of the South are upon you." One of those students, William L. Prather, became president of the new University of Texas in 1899. Remembering the effect of Lee's admonition, in his first Austin speech Prather told the audience, "Students of the University of Texas, the eyes of Texas are upon you." Prather used that line regularly thereafter. Dean T. U. Taylor wrote: "These words soon became familiar to the student body and they were always ready to hear them at the close of an address by the President."

When a minstrel show was planned to raise funds for the Athletic Association, a promoter asked John Lang Sinclair to write a special song. Sinclair complied by satirizing Prather's slogan; fitting those words to the tune of "I've Been Working on the Railroad" he achieved this result:

1. I once did know a President
   Away down south in Texas
   And always, everywhere he went
   He saw the Eyes of Texas

   Chorus: The eyes of Texas are upon you
   All the livelong day
   The eyes of Texas are upon you
   You cannot get away
   Do not think you can escape them
   At night or early in the morn
   The eyes of Texas are upon you
   Till Gabriel blows his horn.

2. Sing me a song of Prexis
   Of days long since gone by
   Again I seem to greet him
   And hear his kind reply.

3. Smiles of gracious welcome
   Before my mem'ry rise
   Again I hear him say to me:
   "Remember Texas' Eyes."

–Ernest Morrison

This copy of the program for the minstrel show at which the "Eyes of Texas" was first performed lists it as simply "a Parody in Song."

Dr. Prather was in the audience at the Hancock Opera House when the minstrel show was held on May 12, 1904. The first public performance of "The Eyes of Texas," listed on the program as "A parody in song," was sung by a quartet composed of J. D. Kivlehen, Ralph A. Porter, W. D. Smith, and James R. Cannon. According to a Dallas *News* account:

> Before the first verse was finished the house was in an uproar and by the time "til Gabriel blows his horn" was reached the audience was semi-hysterical. They pounded the floor and shouted for an encore which the quartet willingly gave again and again and still again until the students themselves were joining with them and the singers were . . . hoarse . . . .

Taylor recalled:

> For two years it was not taken seriously, but the death of William L. Prather in July, 1905, converted "The Eyes of Texas" from minstrel song into the anthem of the University of Texas and the State of Texas. The simple remark of William L. Prather in 1899 has now become the war cry of the University of Texas.

Many Texans believe "The Eyes of Texas" is the state song, a circumstance that caused pain to William J. Marsh, the composer of the official song, "Texas, Our Texas." Dean Taylor, unhappy over the legislature's selection, stated:

> Official bodies can award prizes and pass resolutions that a certain song shall be the State song, but the people that sing the songs will decide what song they will sing. I have heard the labored efforts of the songs that were written for prizes and money, but the song written by a humble poor B. Hall boy in 1903, like Abou Ben Adhem, the Eyes of Texas led all the rest. John Sinclair was a poor boy and the poorest salesman that ever hit Texas when it came to selling himself, but he was a poet of purest ray serene; a patriot of the purest type, who wrote the song not for gold or glory, but to serve his fellow man. And Oh, how he served them.

William L. Prather, a Waco lawyer, became president of the University of Texas in 1899. It was his custom of reminding students that "the eyes of Texas are upon you" which caused John Lang Sinclair to write his famous song.

An Englishman Wrote The State Song

Although William J. Marsh was born in Woolton, England, on June 24, 1880, his mother was a Kentuckian who had met his British father in Dallas while he was employed by the Texas and Pacific Railroad. She taught her son to play the organ, and at the age of sixteen William Marsh succeeded her as the organist for St. Mary's Catholic Church in Woolton. Marsh studied organ and composition in Liverpool and may have attended the Leipsig conservatory, for his teacher, R. W. Oberhoffer, was a respected member of that faculty.

While visiting Texas relatives Marsh was offered a job with the Neil P. Anderson Cotton Company in Fort Worth. Beginning as a bookkeeper in 1904, he worked there for 35 years while pursuing his musical interests. Marsh, a Catholic, was for 36 years the organist at the First Presbyterian Church. He also played the organ at Temple Beth-El Synagogue for 23 years. As organist for St. Patrick's Cathedral, Marsh would, near the close of the 10 o'clock Mass, rush away to the 11 o'clock Presbyterian services; some say his assistant moved onto the bench without missing a note as Marsh departed. For many years Marsh taught at Our Lady of Victory and served as music critic for the Fort Worth *Star-Telegram*.

Most of Marsh's compositions were masses and hymns, but in 1924 he wrote "Texas, Our Texas" for the state song contest announced by Governor Pat Neff. Marsh composed the music and collaborated with Gladys Yoakum Wright on the words.

Since the designation of the bluebonnet as the state flower, Texas governors had been vexed by the submission of proposed state songs. In an effort to end that nuisance—and most of the songs were very bad—Neff sought to provide Texas with an anthem. In his announcement Neff mentioned Robert Burns' desire to write a song for Scotland and quoted an unnamed patriot who stated, "Let me write the songs of a people and I care not who makes their laws."

After referring to the "Marsellaise" of France, England's "God Save the King," and Mexico's "La Paloma," Neff offered "with the aid of generous friends, a prize of one thousand dollars to the person who composes and sets to music a song that shall meet with the approval of a specially appointed" committee and the favor of the legislature in January, 1925.

A sixteen-member committee considered the 286 songs submitted. Some of the composers were from other states; one entry came from Brazil and one from Italy. The committee chose the Marsh song:

1. Texas, Our Texas!
   All hail the mighty State!
   Texas, Our Texas!
   So wonderful—so great!
   Largest and grandest,
   Withstanding every test;
   O Empire, wide and glorious,
   You stand supremely blest.

William J. Marsh, an Englishman who lived in Fort Worth for many years, wrote the state song, "Texas, Our Texas," for a contest to choose an appropriate anthem.

Chorus: God bless you, Texas
         And keep you brave and strong,
         That you may grow in power and worth
         Throughout the ages long.

2. Texas, O Texas!
   Your free-born Single Star
   Sends out her radiance
   To nations near and far.
   Emblem of Freedom!
   It sets our hearts aglow
   With thoughts of San Jacinto
   And glorious Alamo.

3. Texas, dear Texas!
   From tyrant grip now free,
   Shines forth in splendor
   Your Star of Destiny!
   Mother of Heroes!
   We come, your children true,
   Proclaiming our Allegiance—
   Our Faith—Our Love for you!"

Neff congratulated Marsh by telephone, recommended "Texas, Our Texas" to the new legislature, and arranged for its inclusion in new public school textbooks, but his term was ending. On January 20, 1925, Marsh was a special guest at the inauguration of Governor Miriam Ferguson, for "Texas, Our Texas" was then to be performed for the first time at a state event. Unfortunately, as Marsh wrote in the margins of Neff's book describing the event:

Mrs. Ferguson's campaign song, "Put on your old Gray Bonnet" was sung by Mrs. (Ernest O.) Thompson and the Old Grey Mare Band, of Brownwood, . . . played it. But "Texas, Our Texas" was not sung at all. When I met Mrs. Thompson that night at the inaugural ball she said she was waiting to start the new song, but for some reason it never was done. Politics of course!! The Speaker, Satterwhite of Amarillo, was pushing a song by Rade Britain.

Marsh's song was finally adopted on May 23, 1929, as Governor Dan Moody signed the legislative joint resolution. Senator Margie Neal, of Carthage, the chairman of the State Song Committee, had held hearings in each of the 31 Senatorial districts, and Sunset High School hosted the final competition during the 1927 State Fair. "Texas, Our Texas" prevailed over nearly 1,000 entries. Senator Neal, presented the $1,000 check to Marsh. (Marsh noted that Neff never paid the $1,000 he had offered, which really should not have been expected since the 1925 legislature made no adoption. Marsh was grateful that Neff, as president of Baylor, regularly used the state song in chapel services.)

Bandmaster John Phillip Sousa stated that "Texas, Our Texas" was the best of the state songs. Marsh resented the belief of so many people that "The Eyes of Texas" is the official anthem; the Texas State Song Association, based in Fort Worth, has attempted to inform Texans. With $1,000 brought in by a Casa Manana benefit, the organization distributed sheet music of "Texas, Our Texas" to bands and to school children. Fred Pass, of the Dallas *News*, wrote that "Texans should know, at least, what their state song is. Preferably, they should be encouraged to learn to play and sing it."

Marsh, 91 years old, died in 1971 at Fort Worth, never having become an American citizen.

Governor Pat Neff poses with the Old Gray Mare Band of Brownwood at a convention in San Angelo. The band was supposed to perform publicly for the first time "Texas, Our Texas" at the inauguration of Mrs. Ferguson in 1925. The composer was appalled when, instead of the new state song, the band was ordered to play "Put On Your Old Gray Bonnet," the new governor's campaign song.

Bill McDonald Was Woodrow Wilson's Bodyguard

William Jesse McDonald was fourteen years old when his family moved to Rusk County from Mississippi. His Confederate father had been killed at Corinth. In the seventies McDonald was running a Mineola store when he became deputy sheriff and began building a reputation as a peace officer. He operated a lumber yard in Wichita County, then settled on Wanderer's Creek near present Quanah, Hardeman County. For self-protection McDonald obtained a deputy sheriff's commission; a substantial part of the local populace had fled other jurisdictions. McDonald's biographer, Albert Paine, explained:

They were not ordinary malefactors, but choice selections from the world at large. "What was your name before you came to Texas?" was a common inquiry, and it was often added that a man could go to Texas when he couldn't go anywhere else . . . . It was the natural last resort of men who could not live elsewhere with safety or profit. There is a story of a man arrested in Texas in those days for some misdemeanor who was advised to leave the state without delay. "But where shall I go?" asked the troubled offender, "I'm in Texas now!"

The railroad's arrival stimulated Quanah's growth and increased the outlaw population. McDonald was more than a match for them. He became a deputy United States Marshal so he could operate in the Indian Territory. McDonald simply overwhelmed badmen by his daring. He would drive a buckboard up to an outlaw camp and, without conversation, draw on them. At gunpoint he brought in for trial scores of fugitives—as many as six men at a time—sometimes with assistance, sometimes without.

His ranch suffered from neglect, but fees from arrests and contributions from cattlemen's associations brought McDonald's income to a very substantial $500 a month. As a sideline he purchased 200 goats, but the venture was never profitable. The goats escaped into the breaks of the Pease River, and one might spend full-time looking for them. When McDonald ordered a hand to work goats one morning the cowboy stated, "All right, but if you want me to do that, you'll have to get you some goats . . . . There isn't a goat to be found within forty miles."

McDonald said, "I don't care much for goats anyway." Paine noted that Pease River hunters claimed to have killed "mountain sheep" and "antelope," but the animals bore a strong resemblance to McDonald's goats.

In 1891 Governor James Hogg, an old East Texas friend, appointed McDonald commander of Company B of the Rangers' Frontier Battalion. When Theodore Roosevelt announced his intention to hunt wolves in Texas, McDonald was assigned as his bodyguard by Governor S. W. T. Lanham. Removal of the hunt into the Indian Territory—outside his jurisdiction—by hosts W. T. Waggoner and Burk Burnett did not deter McDonald. The Secret Service men turned back at Wichita Falls, where McDonald assumed responsibility for the president's safety. Roosevelt's practice of riding full-gallop over terrain pocked with prairie dog holes distressed McDonald. After Jack Abernathy seized center stage by demonstrating his technique for catching wolves barehanded, Roosevelt attacked a rattlesnake with his riding

Bill McDonald was the archetypal Texas Ranger captain, the "One Riot, One Ranger" lawman.

quirt, fencing with the snake, dodging as it struck, and then stomping it with his boot heel. To prevent a repetition of such hazardous behavior, that night McDonald pitched Roosevelt's quirt into the campfire.

Throughout his career McDonald behaved with consistent fearlessness. Because of his actions in August, 1906, an Army officer involved in a controversy at Fort Brown declared that McDonald would "charge hell with a bucket of water." Ten or twenty armed men believed to be black soldiers of the 25th Infantry had fired into Brownsville homes and businesses, killing one man and injuring another. By the time McDonald and two other Rangers arrived, the townspeople and soldiers constituted separate camps, each expecting attack by the other. When the Army would not surrender the offenders, the Rangers patrolled Fort Brown's entrance to prevent their transfer prior to completion of an investigation. Believing that McDonald did not appreciate the irony of his setting himself in the path of hundreds of angry soldiers, Paine stated: "It may be added that in performance of his duty he would, without a moment's hesitation, have opened fire on all three companies."

McDonald resigned from the Rangers in 1907 and Governor Thomas Campbell made him the State Revenue Agent. Five years later McDonald's friend, Colonel E. M. House, of Houston, was managing Woodrow Wilson's campaign against President William Howard Taft and former president Theodore Roosevelt, the Bull Moose candidate. In October an assassin shot Roosevelt as he left a Milwaukee hotel. The bullet was partially deflected by Roosevelt's spectacles case and the manuscript of the address he was on his way to deliver. Roosevelt protected the gunman until police arrived, gave his speech—which required more than an hour—and collapsed. The other candidates stopped campaigning during his convalescence. Worried about the Democratic nominee's safety, Colonel House sought to give Wilson the kind of protection Roosevelt had received on the wolf hunt. He sent this telegram to McDonald:

"New York, October 15, 1912

Come immediately. Important. Bring your artillery.
E. M. House"

House received this reply:

"Quanah, Texas, October 16, 1912

Coming.
McDonald"

Later, House told a friend:

I merely wired Bill to come at once . . . . He thought I was in trouble so he borrowed a shirt from one of his friends, boarded the train without money (which he borrowed on the way) and landed here in a little over two days after leaving Quanah . . . . He had on his big white Stetson and a four days growth of beard, and I need not tell you he created a sensation . . . .

The mayor and police of one town that I know tried to disarm Bill after he was out of the Ranger Service and had no right to carry arms, but they were unable to accomplish their purpose. I would like to see the New York police try it.

The Ranger and the scholarly Wilson got along well but McDonald, anxious to go home, complained about the paved streets and sidewalks, "Ed, I get awful tired of walking on these rocks."

Colonel House wrote:

The Wilsons were sorry to see him leave. He looked over the Secret Service men to see if he thought them fit. He told me that they did well enough, but he did not

158

like their carrying .38's. When he said this to the Secret Service men, they did not like it and replied, "A .38 will kill a man all right." "Yes," said Bill, "if you give him a week to die in."

Failing to interest O. Henry in writing about McDonald, whose career reflected so much Texas history, House contacted Albert Bigelow Paine, Mark Twain's biographer. They were waiting at New York's New Amsterdam Hotel when McDonald arrived. House wrote:

It was a cold, wet night, and Bill came in with his "slicker" and big Stetson hat. We went upstairs with him. He took off his coat, pulled from one side his .45 and from the other his automatic . . . . I explained to Paine that Bill had to carry his artillery in this way in order to be thoroughly ballasted—that he would have difficulty in walking without it.

One evening at Mark Twain's house:

Mark and Bill were playing billiards and it was amusing to see Bill sight his cue just as if it were a rifle, and three times out of four, send his ball off the table. It entertained Mr. Clemens immensely. When we went upstairs, Clemens ran and Bill ran after, as if to catch him, but did not do so. Bill winked at me and said, "I believe the old man really thinks I could not catch him." Bill is as lean and as agile as a panther.

McDonald, the United States Marshal for the Northern District of Texas by appointment of President Woodrow Wilson, died of pneumonia at Wichita Falls on January 15, 1918.

American Military Aviation Developed at Kelly Field

Although the World War I belligerents regularly used the airplane in combat, by April 6, 1917, when the United States declared war, most American military leaders still considered the air arm's mission to be observation and reconnaissance. General Benjamin Foulois stated, "we had not a single plane that could fire a gun or drop a bomb. There were none that could attain the speed or boast of the maneuverability of those in the air for both sides in Europe." In the rush to make an appropriate effort the Air Service was expanded, and Kelly Field was among the facilities built to train fliers.

John J. Pershing had been aware of European efforts in military aviation since a 1908 trip to France where he talked to Wilbur Wright, who was teaching French officers to fly. As Pershing pursued Pancho Villa in 1916, Captain Benjamin Foulois brought eight planes of the First Aero Squadron into Mexico. Climate, terrain, and use wrecked the planes, and when after a month only two decrepit Jennies remained, Foulois "put a match to them. I didn't want to take a chance that somebody would order us to keep on flying them."

The Signal Corps, at the beginning of 1915, had had 119 pilots and 21 planes. Germany, Russia and France each had 500 airplanes. Germany was spending $45 million a year on military aviation compared to our $250,000. In 1916 Alexander Graham Bell, pointed out that there were only 300 licensed pilots in the country; he advocated an air mail service to produce pilots should the military need them. Of the embarrassing state of American military aviation when war was declared Pershing recalled that the Air Service consisted of 35 pilots, 30 other officers, and 1,000 men, none experienced in handling armaments or bombing systems. The 55 airplanes included 51 declared obsolete and 4 obsolescent by the National Advisory Committee for Aeronautics. Pershing wrote:

> We could not have put a single squadron in the field, although it was estimated later that we should eventually need at least 300 squadrons, each to be composed on the average of some 24 officers, 180 men and 18 aeroplanes . . . .

The French asked for 4,500 American airplanes, 5,000 pilots, and 50,000 mechanics in 1918 and hoped that later the United States could supply 2,000 planes and 4,000 engines monthly.

Ordered to build a new flying field, Foulois in 1916 chose the site on which Kelly Field is situated. Before the land could be acquired legislation was necessary in that the appropriation bill had restricted flying fields to the North and East, a ridiculous provision in view of the fewer days suitable for flying there.

The San Antonio field opened in 1917 and was named for Second Lieutenant George E. M. Kelly, who was the first aviation fatality in Texas. Kelly, born in London, England, on December 14, 1878, had enlisted in the Army in 1903 after attempting to join Canadian and British armies. Commissioned after four years, Kelly served in the Phillipines and China. He tranferred into the aviation section in 1911 and was taught to fly by Glenn Curtiss.

Kelly died on May 10, 1911, in a Curtiss, Type IV, pusher-type biplane with a tricycle landing gear, the Army's second airplane. (The other was a Wright, Type B.) Foulois

Lieutenant G. E. M. Kelly, for whom Kelly Field was named, died in a crash on the parade grounds at Fort Sam Houston in San Antonio.

witnessed the crash at Fort Sam Houston. Kelly made a steep dive toward the ground as he was landing "and hit nose wheel first again. There was a sickening, wrenching sound on impact and I thought the plane would disintegrate right there. But it didn't. Instead, it bounced skyward about 30 feet and headed directly for the line of tents on the far side of the field." Kelly turned to avoid the tents. As the plane hit the ground he was thrown about 20 feet and landed on his head. The refusal of Fort Sam Houston's commanding officer to permit further use of his drill field forced the Army to move its aviation operations to College Park, Maryland. Foulois said, "Kelly died because he was poorly trained, inexperienced, and was flying an unsafe airplane." (The first Army pilot to die in a crash, First Lieutenant Thomas Selfridge, Jr., was killed September 17, 1908; he was the second officer assigned to aeronautical duty, two days after Captain Charles Chandler and five days before First Lieutenant Frank Lahm. Benjamin Foulois was the fourth.)

The climate and terrain that brought Kelly Field to Texas would result in the establishment of these World War I fields: at Fort Worth, Barron Field; at San Antonio, Brooks Field; at Wichita Falls, Call Field; at Fort Worth, Carruthers Field; at Houston, Ellington Field; at Dallas, Love Field; at Waco, Rich Field; and at Fort Worth, Taliaferro Field. Nine of the 27 bases functioning on Armistice Day, November 11, 1918, were in Texas. Many were staffed by units trained at Kelly.

Construction on the 627-acre leased site began in March, 1917. After two months nearly 4,500 officers and men were stationed at Kelly. In May 1,500 contiguous acres became Kelly Field No. 2. In his well-researched thesis William Boden stated:

> The actual flying field was prepared by first cutting the mesquite trees and the cotton plants, then harrowing and leveling the field. As a result of the leveling of the ground and the elimination of the vegetation, a serious dust problem was created. The dust created great damage to the equipment and made living in the area extremely uncomfortable. Oiling the field was suggested as a remedy for the dust, but it was rejected because it was too costly and it might damage future crops if the field was returned to farm use . . . .

The first landings, on April 9, 1917, were made by four planes from Fort Sam Houston flown by Eddie Stinson, Kelly's civilian flying instructor, two officers, and "an unidentified four-foot man." By December Kelly was the Army's largest field, accommodating 32,800 officers and men. Kelly was the Air Service reception center, where recruits awaited shipment to training centers, and in January of 1918, 593 cadets were in flight training; as the only advanced training base, with forty planes in use, Kelly Field was overcrowded. (The first time seven planes were aloft at once rated a story in the San Antonio *Express*.)

The Air Service was separated from the Signal Corps in May of 1918. In the next few years nearly everyone in Army aviation served a tour at Kelly, in the schools for mechanics, cooks, ground officers, and other specialties, as well as during recruit reception and flight instruction. One interesting program trained carrier pigeons, the best medium for sending messages from planes to bases. The birds were released from planes in flight; during training they flew 500 miles a week.

The program for flying officers included about two months of ground school, studying subjects such as flight theory, operation of the airplane, and military courtesy at the University of Texas and seven other institutions. Primary flight training required about five months and enabled the trainee to fly alone, and combat techniques were taught in advanced training.

The Curtiss JN-4D, the Jenny, was used for instruction throughout the war. Twenty-

General Benjamin Foulois, the pioneer of the Army air arm, chose the site and established Kelly Field.

seven men died at Kelly in wartime crashes, but 1,562 pilots were trained, almost twice as many as at Rockwell, the second-ranking base.

After the war Kelly was the Army's sole primary training facility. Ellington was the only other Texas field remaining open after demobilization reduced Army aviation by 95%. Kelly was declared a permanent post in 1922. For awhile all Army flight training was done in Bexar County. Kelly Field Number 2, in 1925, was renamed for Major Thomas Duncan, who was killed at Bolling Field on May 23, 1923. Duncan Field, the headquarters for Air Corps training, was commanded by Brigadier General Frank Lahm, a Wright brothers student and the first to solo in the Army's first airplane in September of 1909.

Among the many famous graduates of Kelly Field were Frank Luke, the World War I ace, Charles Lindbergh, General Claire Chennault, the World War II leader of the Flying Tigers, and Air Force Chief of Staff General Thomas White.

The United States lagged in parachute technology. Germans had used them in World War I, but even after the Armistice pilots died at Kelly Field who could have been saved by parachutes. The first parachute course, developed by Major George Stratemeyer in 1920, was not compulsory since the jumper rode the top wing of an airplane to the proper altitude, pulled the rip cord and let himself be dragged off into space.

Much of the training for Billy Mitchell's experiment pitting airplanes against battleships was done at Kelly. During World War II Duncan became part of Kelly Field. In 1947 the name became Kelly Air Force Base, and by 1967 it occupied more than 3,000 acres and had a work force of 31,000.

-*San Antonio Light*

Charles Lindbergh joined the Army after realizing he had no alternative if he wanted to learn to fly well.

Lindbergh Park was established to commemorate Colonel Charles Lindbergh's service at Kelly Field.

Major General Claire Chennault, commander of the Flying Tigers of World War II, was among those trained at Kelly Field.

Cadet Brooks Died at Kelly Field

Although Americans invented the airplane Europeans made it a military weapon. General Benjamin Foulois wrote:

> When war was declared in 1917, we had done practically nothing on the aviation program even though the war had been going on in Europe since 1914. Up to this time our government had bought 28 airplanes, of which 16 had been wrecked; had trained approximately 40 pilots, of which 11 had been killed.

The Army finally had to develop an air arm when the United States entered World War I. A number of flying fields were opened; Gosport Field was established at San Antonio on May 1, 1917, for the training of flight instructors. A few months later Gosport was renamed to honor the son of a prominent San Antonio jurist, Cadet Sidney Brooks, who died in his final flight before graduation at Kelly Field on November 13, 1917.

Construction began at the 873-acre mesquite-covered site on December 11, 1917. A team of French and American aviators laid out the field, which had sixteen hangars and a dirt flying field. The first plane took off from Brooks Field on March 28, 1918. After the Armistice pilot training ceased at Brooks; in May of 1919 the field became the center for lighter-than-air training. A great hangar was erected to accommodate the Italian-built Roma, a hydrogen-filled craft; however, the dirigible never reached San Antonio. During the flight from Langley Field, Virginia, on February 21, 1922, it hit a power line and exploded. A few months later the hydrogen-filled C-2 brushed the side of the Brooks hangar and blew up. That June lighter-than-air activities were moved from Brooks to Scott Field, Illinois, as heavier-than-air training was concentrated in Bexar County. Brooks had the primary school and advanced training was offered at Kelly, seven miles away.

Early experiments in paratroop warfare were carried out by the Army at Brooks. (General William T. Mitchell had originated the paratrooper idea during World War I.) This new military technique was shown there publicly on April 28, 1929. In a larger demonstration later that year twelve planes flew over and eighteen men jumped. Four minutes after they left their planes at an altitude of 2,000 feet the soldiers had unpacked machine guns from padded containers and were firing. Observers included a Russian field marshal; the U.S.S.R. had been interested in the military possibilities of the parachute for years.

All pilot training was done at Kelly and Randolph fields for several years, but in 1939 Brooks began handling some classes. Brooks trained pilots and observers in World War II. By 1950 the field had grown to 1,280 acres, was headquarters for the 12th Air Force, and had become Brooks Air Force Base. All flight programs ceased at Brooks about the time the medical center was established. On November 21, 1963, the day before his death, John Kennedy dedicated buildings of the Aerospace Medical Division, which furnishes health care and researches medical problems of flight and space.

Cadet Sidney Brooks was killed in a crash at Kelly Field. Brooks Field was named for him.

Randolph Field was the West Point of the Air

In the middle twenties all Army pilots were trained at San Antonio's Brooks and Kelly fields and March Field in California. Facilities and equipment were meager and obsolete; most buildings had been erected for World War I use. General Billy Mitchell's criticism of the nation's under-developed air arm kept President Coolidge from reappointing him as Assistant Chief of the Air Service. Mitchell, a vocal proponent of air power, had embarrassed the Navy by sinking a battleship with bombs dropped from airplanes and had aggravated most high-ranking Army officers with his shrill demands. Reduced to the rank of Colonel and assigned to Fort Sam Houston, Mitchell called a press conference in San Antonio after the Navy dirigible *Shenandoah* crashed in September, 1925. Mitchell denounced the Navy and War departments and was courtmartialed. Benjamin Foulois wrote:

> There were few regular Army officers who sympathized with Mitchell. We were glad that he had focused national attention on the tragic state of our air power but could not condone his methods. General Pershing referred to his conduct as the result of an insidious "Bolshevik bug" which had to be eradicated for the good of the Army. Most of us agreed. The consensus of those who had served with Mitchell and had had to live with his slander and invective was that he had gotten exactly what he deserved.

Coolidge appointed Dwight Morrow to investigate the nation's military aviation. After four weeks of hearings and 100 witnesses the Morrow board recommended expansion of the American air arm. The suggestions were incorporated into the act of July 2, 1926, which created the Army Air Corps and provided for expansion and development of military air power.

General Frank Lahm, the second American military pilot to solo—only a few minutes after the first—commanded the Air Corps Training Center from headquarters at Duncan Field, formerly Kelly Field Number 2. Lahm believed all flight training should be done at one place. Areas adjoining Brooks and Kelly were becoming so well populated neither could expand to accomodate such a major training center; in fact either or both might have to be relocated because of surrounding development.

Bexar County citizens wanted the new training center, especially if Brooks and Kelly were lost. The area had many natural advantages; for instance, only sixteen days a year were unsuitable for flying. On the other hand, San Antonio did not own sufficient land for the installation, as did cities in Florida, Louisiana, and Texas, who offered inducements worth as much as $10 million to obtain the center. The Air Corps preference for San Antonio would be of no consequence unless a 2,000-acre site within ten miles of town could be furnished the Army without charge. Just before the January, 1928, deadline citizens acquired the tract General Lahm had selected near Schertz; the new training center belonged to San Antonio.

The officers responsible for choosing a name had not done so when Captain William M. Randolph, a native of Austin, died in a plane crash at Gorman Field, Texas on February 16, 1928. A 1910 graduate of Texas A & M, Randolph attended the Leon Springs camp in World War I and was adjutant of the Kelly Field Advanced Flying School at the time of his death.

–*Public Information Service, Randolph Field*

This view of Randolph Field from 6,000 feet shows the design of Harold L. Clark, which put the buildings at the center of the base, allowing for runways in three directions.

Lieutenant Harold L. Clark, who drew the plans, placed the buildings at the center of the field, a design which permitted runways in three directions, minimizing wind problems and allowing for expansion. In planning the administration building Clark combined a water tower with offices and other unrelated facilities to create Randolph Field's striking trademark, the "Taj Mahal." The domed, octagonal, 170-foot tower cost less than if each included function had been separately housed. To assist in landscaping, the Daughters of the American Revolution presented 104 live oak trees as part of the George Washington Bicentennial observance.

The dedication in June of 1930 was attended by 15,000 people. It included an air show and parachute jump, but considerable attention was attracted by a fire in Governor Dan Moody's limousine. The big black car halted and the occupants bailed out as smoke poured from beneath the hood. A pumper truck, ready should a plane crash and burn, cut across the field and got stuck, and as the crew tried to free the truck, the limousine exploded. An observer said the "kids got more fun out of watching the governor's car burning up than the fly-by." In his address Governor Moody stated:

> It occurs to me that the future of our whole country may depend on a well-trained Air Corps. All that we are to become may depend on the men who are trained on this field. For it seems to me that the two great lines of defense, the Atlantic and Pacific Oceans, upon which this country has depended in the past, are now gone. It may be that we must depend upon the heroes of the air for the defense of the future.

In late 1931 the Basic Flying School, from Brooks Field, and the Primary School, from March Field, were moved to Randolph. Flight training was in three stages: the cadet soloed in primary, in basic he flew more sophisticated planes, and in advanced training—at Kelly Field—he specialized in pursuit, bomber, or transport aircraft. Upon graduation the cadet was commissioned and given his wings. For the next twenty years, Randolph Field's main mission was training pilots and instructors. The class system was utilized, with basic cadets acting as upperclassmen and disciplining those in the primary program. Called "the West Point of the Air," Randolph Field captured the public interest and was used as the setting for several movies such as "I Wanted Wings."

As Hitler began his conquest of Europe, the Air Corps was expanded. Civilian contract schools took over primary training, while Randolph concentrated on basic. To assure that the private schools gave uniform training, Randolph offered a course for primary instructors. When the goal for Army pilot production was raised to 7,000, in 1939, nine new contract schools were added and two training centers—Maxwell Field, Alabama, and Moffett Field, California—were established to assist Randolph. During World War II, as annual pilot quotas grew to 12,000 and then 30,000, Randolph Field trained instructors for the entire Air Corps. Near the close of the war the Central Instructors School was moved to Waco, and Randolph trained heavy bomber crews. After the war pilot training once more was the main mission. Between 1931 and 1943 and from 1946 to 1951 Randolph Field graduated 15,396 pilots. The Central Instructors School produced 12,585 pilot instructors.

Crew training became the primary mission in 1952. The change to jet bombers was effected by mid-decade and Randolph Air Force Base had only one B-29 by 1956, although 21,000 airmen had learned about the Superfortress there. Training for KC-97 tanker crews became the main responsibility in 1958.

Early in World War I, the British learned the importance of physical and mental standards, for only 2% of their flying casualties were caused by the enemy, 8% resulted from

–*Public Information Service, Randolph Field*

The circle in front of the main building—the "Taj Mahal"—at Randolph Air Force Base.

airplane defects, and 90% of the deaths of British pilots were attributable to physical or psychological deficiencies. Obviously an air service needed some way to exclude those likely to destroy themselves and their equipment. The location of the School of Aviation Medicine at Randolph permitted physical and psychological standards to be developed and enforced; it also afforded opportunities for the study of large numbers of trainees. In 1959 the School of Aviation Medicine was relocated at Brooks Air Force Base.

Captain William R. Randolph was killed in a plane crash at Gorman Field, Texas. Randolph Field was named for him.

A typical Randolph Field publicity shot during the time when movies set at the "West Point of the Air" were current.

Some visitors stand on the wings of a Randolph Field training plane and encourage a cadet to solo.

Eastland's Old Rip Slept 31 Years

Eastland County, created two years before, had only 99 residents, mostly stock farmers, by 1860; it was not organized for another thirteen years. The first county seat, Merriman, was simply the headquarters of Flannegan's Ranch. In 1874 Charles Connellee platted Eastland with the intention of making it the county seat. The county government took up residence in the second story of Connellee's building after an August, 1875, election. Connellee gave the courthouse square and enough additional land to finance a rock capitol and a calaboose Eastland boosters called the "finest jail west of Fort Worth."

A new courthouse took the place of the rock building in 1897; when that temple of justice was demolished, in 1928, a live horned frog was found imprisoned in its cornerstone. Named for Rip Van Winkle, who slept twenty years, the toad became a national celebrity through publicity generated by Boyce House, the Eastland *Argus-Tribune* editor and author of many Texas books. Old Rip appeared in Robert Ripley's "Believe It or Not" cartoon feature and became the first Texas reptile to meet an incumbent American president.

A heated controversy ensued concerning the toad's survival for 31 years without food or water which has never been resolved. Apparently most Eastland citizens believed the statements of eyewitnesses who swore that no one could have tampered with the contents of the hollow cornerstone; however, others considered Rip's longevity impossible.

The horned frog is really a lizard. Although armored and spiked, they are shy and harmless; their main defensive technique is the ejection of blood through the eyes. Horned toads—tough and proud—were so plentiful on the Waco campus Texas Christian University named its athletic teams for them. The undefeated 1938 Horned Frogs were the first from the Southwest Conference to win the national collegiate football championship, and David O'Brien, the 145-pound quarterback, an All American, was the first Heisman trophy winner from Texas.

Horned frogs have a life span of three or four years; however, old timers in West Texas vowed that one of the toads could live a century without food or water. Newspaper stories told of frogs spending years in a state of suspended animation.

Ernest Wood, Eastland's County Clerk, decided to test the horned frog's ability to endure. In 1897 on that summer day when the cornerstone of the new courthouse was to be leveled, he came home for lunch and found his son, Will, playing with a horned toad; when he returned downtown Wood took the lizard with him and had it placed inside the cornerstone.

That a horned frog was sealed inside the stone was a well-known local belief and as the courthouse was being demolished more than thirty years later, House reminded his readers of Wood's tale. On February 18, 1928, about 1,500 spectators gathered for the opening of the cornerstone, and Ernest Wood called out, "If there is a horned frog in there, it's mine." Boyce House wrote:

> A jagged wall of brick, eight feet high, still stood above the stone. A chain was looped about the wall and a truck (to which the chain was attached) began to pull. So firmly was the wall cemented to the cornerstone that not only did the

Blair Cherry, who would later be head coach at the University of Texas, holds Old Rip immediately after he was removed from the cornerstone of the old Eastland County courthouse.

wall but also the stone began to yield . . . . when the pulling was resumed, the brick wall fell, leaving the cornerstone in place.

A Methodist minister, the Reverend F. E. Singleton, and other clergymen were present to bolster credence in whatever occurred. As the workmen raised the metal plate covering the hole in the top of the stone, Singleton, who had shed his coat and rolled up his sleeves despite the cold, announced that he could see a frog. Eugene Day reached in, picked up the dusty toad, which was dead or asleep, and handed it to Singleton. Then County Judge Ed Pritchard held the horned frog over his head, and as the crowd cheered it began to wake. Ranger football coach Blair Cherry, who later coached at the University of Texas, was photographed holding Old Rip, who had exceeded Rip Van Winkle's record of two decades by nearly eleven years.

Because of the Boyce House stories, which had been reprinted all over the nation, Ernest Wood received numerous requests for appearances by Rip. The Eastland paper reported:

> The crowds continue to pour into the city to view the noted toad and enterprising photographers are reaping much money from postal cards bearing Rip's picture. Meanwhile the frog sits in a display window blinking at the queer faces of some of the thousands who peer in at him. He appears to be in no hurry to break his fast of 31 years and to date has not eaten any foods although tempting morsels of bugs, worms and grass have been placed before him.

Will Wood recalled that the frog was "as thin as a match" when removed from the cornerstone. "It was five or six weeks before he took anything to eat and equally as long before he could move himself along on his legs. An x-ray showed a leg broken and a few other minor injuries, but outside of that he was all right."

Will Wood took him on tour; Rip traveled in a bowl filled partially with sand. At Dallas they were delayed because of a writ of attachment forbidding Rip's removal pending trial of a suit in which a local man sought damages for Wood's refusal to allow him to exhibit the frog. The Dallas Chamber of Commerce posted a $1,000 bond, and Wood, fearing additional legal problems, hurried out of town carrying Rip in a brown paper sack.

Rip attracted huge crowds in Royce City and Greenville, and 10,000 turned out at Sulphur Springs. An April 30 newspaper story reported that doubts of Rip's authenticity did not diminish attendance in St. Louis, where 40,000 people viewed the toad one day.

> So many people came to see him yesterday that special guards were called to dissolve the blockades. Attendants at the reptile house had expected unusual crowds, but not for St. Louis to come out in a body to see Old Rip. Some persons jeered at the placard over the glass case in which the toad was exhibited which set forth that Rip lived 31 years without air or water or food. But scoffers and believers alike came to see the small reptile which seemed not at all perturbed by the thousands of eyes that peered at him.

The St. Louis Zoological Society paid to exhibit Rip, and its president offered a thousand dollars to anyone who could disprove his story. The crowd became unruly when attendants attempted to close the building at the end of the day.

Wood took Rip to Washington, where Dr. William T. Hornaday, the former director of the New York Zoological Gardens, was to have him examined. Senator Earle B. Mayfield, of Texas, arranged for Rip to visit the White House, and newspapers noted that Calvin Coolidge "stroked the frog's back with his horned-rimmed glasses, and then the President and Old Rip gazed steadily at each other for a full minute without a sound—Silent Cal had met his match." In New York a movie was made about Rip. House reported:

> A horned frog's favorite food consists of red ants; this delicacy was not available in Manhattan but a professional bug catcher provided a suitable substitute, at

–F. James Dabney

This photograph of the ceremonies at the present county capitol is inscribed "Laying cornerstone of Eastland County courthouse, May 12, 1928 by International Order of Oddfellows Grand Lodge of Texas." A live horned frog was put inside that cornerstone, but a court order was issued the following day setting it free. Man with raised arm is holding a horned frog.

fifty cents per bug, and the cameras showed Rip feasting.

Rip died of pneumonia on January 19, 1929, after a norther hit Eastland. Embalmed and placed in a satin-lined coffin donated by the National Casket Company, after several years Rip was put on display in a special glass case in the courthouse.

Old Rip's mortal remains have suffered somewhat in the past 50 years. Gubernatorial candidate John Connally allegedly broke off a leg when a local supporter handed Rip to him in 1962; actually the injury occurred years before when Wood's small daughter was showing the frog to a friend.

On January 16, 1973, Rip was "frognapped." The substitution of imposter toads provoked the kidnapper to write a letter which James Dabney quoted in the Abilene *Reporter-News* on March 30, 1974:

> To the public. The purpose of this writing is to clarify the mystery surrounding the disappearance of Old Rip . . . . I . . . am the person who removed Old Rip from public display and he definitely remains in my possession as the enclosed photograph should establish beyond any doubt . . . . I had planned to remain silent but this attempt to keep "the legend of Old Rip" alive by replacing him with an obvious fake has forced me to tell my story.
>
> I am one of three surviving perpetrators of the hoax which grew into "the legend of Old Rip." One evening some 45 years ago five young men, including myself, decided to place a live horned frog in the cornerstone in the old courthouse which had just been demolished. With a little help from a member of the demolition crew we were able to lift the cornerstone and toss the horned toad inside. The cornerstone was reopened the next day at the ceremoney . . . . we were all surprised at the amount of excitement caused by our prank . . . . However, in recent years I have become increasingly regretful of our actions so long ago. I have seen various community leaders and organizations eagerly exploiting Old Rip and neglecting many civic responsibilities which are so vital to a small town today.

Hoping to keep Eastland from "building its future around a dried-up horned frog" the writer stole Old Rip, but:

> Several days later I was dismayed to learn that a new Old Rip had appeared in the courthouse. I proceeded to remove this rather poor imitation and the coffin lay empty for almost a year. Nevertheless another fake was produced last week during the livestock show. I then realized it was useless to continue abducting all the imposter Old Rips and the only way to end it was by telling the truth once and for all.

He promised to return the original Rip by mail upon removal of the imposter.

Some doubters thought the contractor for the new courthouse had perpetrated the fraud, but James Golden stated that he and fifteen or twenty others remained by the cornerstone all night prior to the opening "to see to it that there wasn't no hanky panky." Railway Express agent H. A. McCanlies moved to Eastland in 1921 and rented a house from E. E. Wood, who told him then about the criticism he had received through the years for placing the toad in the cornerstone. McCanlies explained, "He, like myself and other folks had always heard that a horned frog would live a hundred years or more if it could find an airtight space."

When the old courthouse was to be torn down everyone looked forward to the settlement of the question of the longevity of toads. McCanlies, only a few feet away when Rip was removed, recalled that a section of wall ten feet high still remained above the cornerstone that morning, and even after it was toppled workmen had to pry away brick and mortar to uncover an airtight lead seal. McCanlies said Rip looked like a piece of bark off an oak tree. "The

This is the way the Eastland County courthouse looks today. In the foreground is the cornerstone from the old courthouse in which Old Rip was found. Below the window is a pedestal with Old Rip's name on it and inside the glass case rests the last mortal remains of the toad or one of his successors.

Reverend held him by the tail and then after a moment his legs began to move and after a few deep breaths of air he began to fill out and look like a frog again. He was then placed in the south sunlit window of Madden's drugstore . . . ." Since "horned frogs hibernate from early winter until the latter part of April or the middle of May it would have been impossible for anyone to have obtained the frog and placed him in the stone as claimed by some people."

Edward Cox wrote of the opening:

> I then saw one of the party reach down and bring to sight a horned frog which seemingly was dormant, but after a few moments showed signs of life. A man sitting on the ground between the cornerstone and Mr. Frost and myself got up, brushed his pants with his hand and as he passed remarked, "Well I be damned, if I had not seen it I would not have believed it." That was about how the writer felt about it.

A few months after Rip's discovery, workmen tearing down a fifteen-year-old wall at San Antonio's Gunter Hotel found a toad which was "as flat as a pancake and covered with a hard crust of mortar." The frog was barely able to move, but hotel personnel hoped "by soaking it in water" to restore it to normal, according to the Dallas *News*. In 1930 the Oklahoma State Historical Society Museum displayed three live toads taken from a Beaver County Indian mound. J. B. Thoburn, the museum curator, and two other archeologists believed them to be 300 to 400 years old. Scientists of the Museum of Natural History in Washington were unconvinced after a staff member inspected the Oklahoma toads and declared that "an animal doesn't live forever or even half of forever."

For several years an Eastland Horned Frog celebration was held, usually presided over by Boyce House, who would return for the big event, a race in which competing toads were placed in a ring and the fleetest—the first one out—won $100 or so for its owner.

Rip's celebrity was bad for the horned frog community. Tourists bought them by the thousands for souvenirs. Eastland filling stations gave them away as premiums. In June, 1928, the president of the Dallas Lions Club advertised in Ranger that he would pay 10¢ each for toads. When hordes of kids with hordes of frogs—one had 234—responded, he dropped the price to 2½¢ each. An outraged father attached the Dallasite's truck and 1,200 frogs as he sued in the justice court for $197.25, the balance due his son at 10¢ per frog. Texas' horned frog population has declined severely in the past half century, although some protection is afforded by a statute making the collection and sale of the toads a misdemeanor.

A live horned toad was placed inside the cornerstone of the present Eastland County courthouse, but outraged citizens freed him the next day.

Old Rip at the peak of his fame. After his death he was embalmed at the Hamner Funeral Home. For several years before he was put on display at the Eastland Courthouse, he was kept in a drawer at the home of Will Wood.

The horned frog as seen through the window in front of the courthouse. This is an imposter substituted after Old Rip was kidnapped.

–F. James Dabney

This photograph of Old Rip was taken on March 28, 1972 after he had been taken from the Eastland County Courthouse. The film was sent by the anonymous frognapper to F. James Dabney, who developed and printed it.

This photograph was sent to F. James Dabney by the perpetrator of the Old Rip kidnapping. Showing the horned frog that was substituted after Rip was kidnapped, it demonstrated possession of Rip and the first imposter toad. (The authentic Old Rip had lost part of his leg.) The culprit promised to return the original when the people of Eastland stopped putting phonies on display.

–Texas Christian University

T.C.U. began using the horned frog as a mascot because they were so plentiful on the Waco campus. The T.C.U. Horned Frogs were the first national collegiate football champions from Texas, in 1938, and their 145-pound quarterback, David O'Brien, won the Heisman Trophy.

Enid Justin Sponsored a Pony Express Race

Some recovery had been realized by 1939, but the Great Depression still was the main fact of economic life. Texans had stimulated activity with the 1936 Centennial at Dallas; now New York and San Francisco were staging world's fairs. These events benefited local and national economies. On a lesser scale walkathons, flagpole sitters, dance marathons, bank nights and a thousand other promotions were utilized to create jobs and encourage spending. Enid Justin, the founder and owner of the Nocona Boot Company, decided to make something happen and to sell some boots in the process. She would sponsor a pony express race from Nocona, Texas, to the fairgrounds of the Golden Gate International Exposition 2,000 miles away in San Francisco. Billed as the longest horse race in history, its winner would receive 750 new silver dollars from the San Francisco mint.

On March 1, 1939, Amon Carter, publisher of the *Fort Worth Star-Telegram* and West Texas booster, fired a pistol signaling the start of the race and 5,000 people watched seventeen cowboys and one cowgirl gallop down Nocona's main thoroughfare, California-bound. Some of the contestants soon dropped out. The twelve who made serious efforts to finish were Shannon Davidson, of Matador; King Kerley, of Quanah; George Cates, of Crowell; Shorty Hudson, of Knox City; T. J. Sykes, of Debo, Oklahoma; Chris Uselton, of Nocona; Bob Boyer, of Crowell; Jack Clifton, of McLean; Hudie Hems, of Dumas; Lige Reed, of Electra; Slim Mathis, of Dalhart; and D. H. Henderson, of San Angelo. The only non-Texan, Sykes, had a good lead but one of his horses gave out just east of El Paso. Eight men finished the race.

One of the favorites, Cates, periodically would run a mile to save his mounts. His father had ridden for the original pony express. Near Los Angeles one of his horses foundered, but the judges allowed Cates to stay in the race with one pony and to run the 25-mile stretches the other would have covered. (The rationale was that riders for the old pony express continued on foot if a horse failed.) Cates finished third.

Uselton was in second place and threatening to take the lead when a car struck him and his horse in Ventura, California, and he had to withdraw because of injuries.

The winner was Matador cowboy Shannon Davidson, 22 years old, who crossed the finish line in downtown Oakland at 2 p.m. on March 24. Kerley was second, arriving at 10 a.m. on March 25, and Cates came in third at 2 o'clock that afternoon.

Each contestant bought $25 worth of Pony Express commemorative stamps upon entering the race, and he was supplied with programs, photographs of riders, postcards, souvenir horseshoes and other such items, which were to be sold along the route to cover the expenses of riders, animals and helpers. Every contestant was given a mail bag similar to those used by the original pony express in which he carried letters bearing the 3¢ San Francisco fair commemorative stamp and the Pony Express stamp, which was cancelled with the imprint "Nocona, Texas, 9 a.m. March 1, 1939." The Golden Gate International Exposition stamp was to be cancelled in San Francisco with the date and hour of the winner's arrival in Oakland.

Each contestant was to use two horses, alternating them every 25 miles. At the pony express stations set up along the course the crew got the fresh horse ready, loaded the other

–Enid Justin

Enid Justin, the owner of the Nocona Boot Company and sponsor of the 1939 Pony Express Race to California, fits Chris Uselton for boots. Others, left to right, are J. C. Gentry, Joe Myers, and Dave Gardner.

into a trailer, and drove to the next station. The riders were to judge how many times a day each mount could be worked. Every horse had an identification cable around its neck, closed by a seal, to insure that the same animals were used throughout the race. The contestants were not permitted to cross the Bay Bridge on horseback, for it was believed that the rhythm of an animal's gait might collapse the span. From Oakland the horses were taken by truck to the fairgrounds on Treasure Island.

Late in the race the Society for the Prevention of Cruelty to Animals announced it would investigate Davidson for alleged cruelty to his horses by riding them such a long distance. Davidson snapped, "I take better care of these horses than I do myself." The investigation was soon abandoned.

Enid Justin's father, H. J. Justin, of Lafayette, Indiana, had been a bootmaker in Gainesville and, beginning in 1879, at Spanish Fort. He moved his shop to Nocona upon the arrival of the railroad there. Miss Justin and her brothers grew up in the boot business. Her schooling ended in the eighth grade when she admitted dancing at her brother's 21st birthday party the night before. Suspended for three weeks by her teacher, she told him, "Anybody thinks that there is a party going on in my own house and I'm going upstairs to bed has something else to think about." She never considered returning. "Why Daddy Joe and Mother didn't make me go back to school, I don't know. But I'm grateful to my father every day of my life for giving me the opportunity he gave my brothers."

When her brothers moved the business—H. J. Justin and Sons—to Fort Worth in 1925, she refused to go. Ignoring their dire warning, she started her own firm; on the 50th birthday of the Nocona Boot Company her 350 employees were making 1,500 pairs of boots a day.

Fort Worth Star-Telegram publisher Amon Carter came to Nocona to help Miss Justin start the race.

The pony express contestants leave Nocona, headed for the San Francisco World's Fair.

T. J. Sykes, of Debo, Oklahoma, was the only non-Texan in the race to California.

Chris Uselton, of Nocona, was in second place in the pony express race when he was hit by a car in Ventura, California.

The end of the race. Shannon Davidson, of Matador, the winner, rides through Oakland, the city founded by Texas Ranger Jack Hays, behind a police car.

Amarillo is the Helium Capital

Helium, the second most common element in the universe, is in relatively short supply on earth. Since 90% of the free world's known helium reserves are located within 250 miles of Potter County and the nearby Cliffside field was so important in utilization of the element, the 1968 helium centennial was celebrated in Amarillo.

On October 20, 1868, Sir Norman Lockyer, then a British War Office Clerk and part-time astronomer, discovered helium in the sun's chromosphere. Using a spectroscope Lockyer found in the spectrum of the sun a yellow line with which he was unfamiliar and assumed it to be evidence of the presence of an element which did not exist on earth. He named the element helium, *helios* meaning sun in Greek.

Later W. F. Hillebrand, of the United States Department of the Interior, while working with Uranite obtained a gas he could not identify. In 1895 Sir William Ramsay, of the University of London, aware of Hillebrand's work, extracted a similar gas from Clevite. After removing oxygen and nitrogen Ramsay found the residue was helium.

Although it had been shown that helium existed on earth, there was no suggestion of its presence in quantities useful to man until in 1903 Dr. Hamilton Cady discovered a gas sample from a Dexter, Kansas, well to be 2% helium. Cady also found helium in other Kansas wells. When Cady's student, Clifford Seibel, read a paper on helium before the American Chemical Society in 1917, the world took notice, for World War I belligerents were fighting in the air as well as upon the ground. Hydrogen-filled balloons and dirigibles exploded; helium had as much lifting power and was not flammable.

The British wanted to use helium-filled barrage balloons for protection against German dirigibles used as bombers, but they had no helium and, as Dr. Anthony Davison, of the University of Kansas put it, "The entire American supply, perhaps half a cubic foot, lay on a shelf in Dr. Cady's laboratory, and the cost of production was estimated at about $2,500 a cubic foot." (Through Seibel's work helium would be produced at the rate of a billion cubic feet a year and a cost of 3½¢ a foot.)

Pressed by the British, the United States tried to develop helium for military use. The Dexter field was nearly depleted, but the Petrolia oil field near Wichita Falls, opened in 1903, produced gas containing .84% helium which was sold in Dallas and Fort Worth by Lone Star Gas Company. The Bureau of Mines, acting for the Navy, supervised the building of two privately-owned helium plants adjoining Lone Star's metering plant in north Fort Worth; they began operating in the spring of 1918.

For security reasons the word "helium" was not used; instead the product was "X gas," or "argon." Troops from Camp Bowie guarded the plants. Dr. Seibel left the University of Kansas to run the Bureau of Mines laboratory at Fort Worth. Helium did not play a significant part in the war, but the plants demonstrated the possibility of its extraction. The experimental units were closed in January 1919, but permanent helium plants operated in Fort Worth from 1921 to 1929. When a larger facility was projected a new source was required and only one was adequate, the 50,000-acre Cliffside field near Amarillo, where the gas was 1.5% helium.

The Helium Centennial monument in Amarillo is composed of four time capsules sealed in helium to be opened at intervals within the next thousand years.

On December 7, 1921, the Navy's C-7, made by the Goodyear Tire and Rubber Company, was filled with helium produced during the war and became the first such craft ever flown. Seibel illustrated the significant military consequences by quoting remarks by Texas congressman Lucien Parish, who recalled that the zepplin bombardment of factories and rail points had a substantial effect upon Allied morale: "Of the 90 or more airships used by the Germans during the war, 22 were shot down, 6 others burned, but the remaining 62 were able to write their record of terror in the hearts of the people of the surrounding territory."

In 1925 the Helium Conservation Act put production responsibility in the Bureau of Mines. Arrangements were made for an 18-acre plant site just outside Amarillo. Operations began in 1929. Residue gas from the plant was sold to a zinc smelter. The cost of Amarillo-produced helium was much lower than that from the Fort Worth Bureau of Mines plant which had been closed.

As the age of dirigibles passed helium demand fell, and helium became available for commercial use in 1937. With World War II expansion of the Navy's lighter-than-air arm, the Bureau of Mines built four new plants. The product's purity was raised from 98.2% to 99.995% to fulfill requirements imposed by new uses. Demand grew rapidly and by 1975 there were 12 plants in the United States—only two government operated—and one in Canada. Except for Canada, France, the U.S.S.R. and Eastern Europe, the United States is the only substantial helium producer.

The helium atom is composed of two electrons orbiting a nucleus of two protons and two neutrons. Chemically the most inert element, helium cannot be combined with another element at any temperature. It is extracted from natural gas at 300° below zero; after other elements have become liquid, helium is drawn off as a gas. (Even at 450° below zero helium does not freeze.) Helium is transported under pressure in stainless steel containers; extremely light, 1,000 cubic feet of helium will lift 66 pounds.

Most helium is used by industry; however, it is essential to the space program. Astronauts breathe a mixture of oxygen and helium; to get used to extreme temperatures they drill in helium-filled rooms at temperatures of 225° below zero. In rockets such as Atlas and Saturn V, helium provides pressure to force liquid fuel into engines and prevent collapse of empty tanks. Helium is used in arc welding and testing for minute leaks in such products as refrigerators. Helium detection devices can reveal holes so small that 3,000 years would be required for a liter of air to leak out through them. Helium is mixed with oxygen for deep penetration into lungs of patients with respiratory ailments and with anesthetic gases to reduce the risk of operating room explosions.

The reason for the Amarillo area's helium is the Cap Rock beneath the Llano Estacado, or Staked Plain. Helium is present in natural gas found elsewhere, but quantities are small because most has escaped through the porous materials covering it. On the other hand, the Cap Rock—which is not a rock but a layer of highly mineral particles that have cemented themselves together—is as non-porous as granite or marble and retains helium until a well is drilled through it.

The Helium Time Columns Monument was erected in Amarillo during the centennial. Three of the stainless steel columns form a tripod supporting the fourth, which extends vertically 55 feet above the slate base. The tubes contain some 4,000 items stored in helium. (The Declaration of Independence and the Constitution on display at the Library of Congress are also sealed in helium.) The first column is to be opened in 25 years, the next in 50 years, the third in 2068 A.D. and the last in the year 2968.

References

Books

Bancroft, Hubert Howe. *History of the North Mexican States and Texas.* San Francisco: 1884-1889.

Barton, Henry W. *Texas Volunteers in the Mexican War.* Wichita Falls: By the author, 1970.

Bell, Thomas W. *A Narrative of the Capture and Subsequent Sufferings of the Mier Prisoners in Mexico.* Waco: Texian Press, 1964.

Benavides, Alonso de. *The Memorial of Fray Alonso de Benavides, 1630;* Translated by Mrs. Edward M. Ayer, Annotated by Frederick Hodge and Charles Lummis. Chicago: 1916.

Benet, Stephen Vincent. *John Brown's Body.* New York: Holt, Rinehart and Winston, 1968.

Biographical Directory of the Texan Conventions and Congresses. Austin: Book Exchange, Inc., 1941.

Bolton, Herbert. *Athanase De Mézières and the Louisiana-Texas Frontier, 1768-1780.* Cleveland: The Arthur C. Clark Co., 1914.

Bolton, Herbert. *Texas in the Middle of the Eighteenth Century.* Austin: University of Texas Press, 1970.

Branch, Hetty. *The Story of 80 John.* New York: Greenwich, 1960.

Brendt, L. W. "Helium," *Encyclopedia of the Chemical Elements.* New York: Reinhold Book Corp., 1968.

Brown, John Henry. *Indian Wars and Pioneers of Texas.* Austin: L. E. Daniell, 1848.

Carter, Hodding. *Doomed Road of Empire.* New York: McGraw-Hill Book Company, 1963.

Carter Capt. R. G. *On the Border with Mackenzie.* New York: Antiquarian Press, Ltd., 1961.

Castañeda, Carlos. *Our Catholic Heritage in Texas*, Vol. I. Austin: Von Boeckmann-Jones Co., 1936.

Chabot, Frederick C. *With the Makers of San Antonio.* San Antonio: By the author, 1937.

Chandler, Charles deForest, and Lahm, Frank P. *How Our Army Grew Wings, Airmen and Aircraft before 1914.* New York: The Ronald Press, 1943.

Chatfield, Lt. W. H. *The Twin Cities of the Border.* New Orleans: E. P. Brandao, 1893.

Cox, Edwin T. *History of Eastland County.* San Antonio: The Naylor Company, 1950.

Davis, Ellis, and Grobe, Edwin, editors. *Encyclopedia of Texas.* Dallas: Texas Development Bureau, no date.

Dawson, Joseph. *José Antonio Navarro.* Waco: Baylor University Press, 1969.

Day, James M. *Black Beans and Goose Quills.* Waco: Texian Press, 1970.

Domínguez, Fray Francisco Atanasi. *The Missions of New Mexico, 1776.* Albuquerque: University of New Mexico Press, 1956.

Evans, Joe. *Bloys Cowboy Camp Meeting.* El Paso: Guynes Printing Co., 1959.

Falconer, Thomas. *Letters and Notes on the Texan Santa Fe Expedition, 1841-1842.* Chicago: Rio Grande Press, 1963.

Finck, Sr. Mary Helena. *The Congregation of the Sisters of Charity of the Incarnate Word, San Antonio, Texas.* Washington, D.C.: Catholic University of America, 1925.

Foreman, Grant. *Marcy and the Gold Seekers*. Norman: University of Oklahoma Press, 1968.

Ford, John Salmon. *Rip Ford's Texas*. Austin: University of Texas Press, 1963.

Forrest, Earle R. *Missions and Pueblos of the Southwest*. Cleveland: The Arthur Clark Co., 1929.

Foulois, Major General Benjamin D. *From the Wright Brothers to the Astronauts, The Memoirs of Major General Benjamin D. Foulois with Colonel C. V. Glines, USAF*. New York: McGraw Hill Book Company, 1968.

Morfi, Fray Juan Agustín. *History of Texas, 1673 to 1779*. Albuquerque: Quivira Society, 1935.

Gibson, A. M. *The Kickapoos: Lords of the Middle Border*. Norman: University of Oklahoma Press, 1963.

Gibson, John M. *Physician to the World, the Life of General William C. Gorgas*. Durham, North Carolina: Duke University Press, 1950.

Gittinger, Theodore; Rihn, Connie; Haby, Roberta; and Snavely, Charlene. *St. Louis Church, Castroville*. San Antonio: Graphic Arts, 1973.

Gorgas, Marie D. and Hendrick, Burton J. *William Crawford Gorgas, His Life and Work*. Garden City, New York: Doubleday and Company, 1924.

Gorgas, William Crawford. *Sanitation in Panama*. New York: D. Appleton and Co., 1915.

Grant, U. S. *Personal Memoirs of U. S. Grant*. New York: Charles L. Webster and Co., 1885.

Gray, Colonel William F. *Diary of Col. William F. Gray, From Virginia to Texas, 1835*. Houston: Fletcher Young Publishing Co., 1965.

Green, General Thomas J. *Journal of the Texian Expedition Against Mier*. New York: Harper and Brothers, 1845.

Greer, James Kimmins. *Colonel Jack Hays*. New York: E. P. Dutton & Co., 1952.

Hackett, C. W. and Shelby, C. C., editors. *Revolt of the Pueblo Indians of New Mexico and Otermin's Attempted Reconquest, 1680-1682*, 2 vols. Albuquerque: Coronodo Historical Series, 1942.

Hamilton, Holman. *Zachary Taylor, Soldier of the Republic*. Indianapolis: Bobbs-Merrill Co., 1941.

Havins, T. R. *Something About Brown*. Brownwood: Banner Printing Co., 1958.

Hay, Kenneth. *The Life and Influence of Charles Carlton*, By the author, 1939.

Hendrix, John. *If I Can Do It Horseback*. Austin: University of Texas Press, 1964.

Hedrick, V. P. *The Grapes of New York*. Albany: J. B. Lyon Co., State Printers, 1908.

Henry, William S. *Campaign Sketches of the War with Mexico*. New York: Harper and Bros., 1847.

A History of Ward County, Texas. Texas Permian Historical Society, editors. Monahans: Monahans Junior Chamber of Commerce, 1962.

Hodge, Floy Grandell. *A History of Fannin County*. Hereford: Pioneer Publishers, 1966.

Hodge, Frederick Webb, editor. *Handbook of American Indians North of Mexico*. Smithsonian Institution, Bureau of American Ethnology, Bulletin 30, Volume II, Washington, D.C.: U.S. Government Printing Office, 1910.

Holden, William Curry. *Alkali Trails or Social and Economic Movements of the Texas Frontier, 1846-1900*. Dallas: The Southwest Press, 1930.

Hollon, W. Eugene and Butler, Ruth Lapham, editors. *William Bollaert's Texas*. Norman: University of Oklahoma Press, 1956.

House, Boyce. *Cowtown Columnist*. San Antonio: The Naylor Company, 1946.

Hunter, J. Marvin, editor. *Jack Hays, The Intrepid Texas Ranger*. Bandera: Bandera Press, 1937.

Jacks, L. V. *Claude Dubuis, Bishop of Galveston*. St. Louis: B. Herder Book Co., 1947.

Johnson, Frank W. *A History of Texas and Texans*, Eugene C. Barker, editor. Chicago: American Historical Society, 1914.

Johnston, J. E. *San Antonio to El Paso, Fort Smith to Santa Fe*. Washington, D.C.: 1850.

Kendall, George Wilkins. *Narrative of the Texan Santa Fe Expedition*, Vol. I & II. New York: Harper and Bros., 1844.

Koelling, Gordon and Balazik, Ronald. "Helium." *Mineral Facts and Problems, 1975*. Washington, D.C.: U. S. Government Printing Office, 1975.

La Torre, Felipe and Delores. *The Mexican Kickapoo Indians*. Austin: University of Texas Press, 1976.

Lea, Tom. *The King Ranch*. Boston: Little Brown and Co., 1957.

Leckie, William. *The Buffalo Soldiers*. Norman: University of Oklahoma Press, 1967.

Lipper, Harold. "Helium." *Mineral Facts and Problems, 1965*. Bulletin 630. Washington, D.C.: U. S. Government Printing Office, 1965.

Lockhart, John. *Sixty Years on the Brazos*. Waco: Texian Press, 1967.

Loomis, Noel. *The Texan-Santa Fe Pioneers*. Norman: University of Oklahoma Press, 1958.

Lord, Walter, editor. *The Fremantle Diary, Being the Journal of Lieutenant Colonel James Arthur Lyon Fremantle, Coldstream Guards, and his Three Months in the Southern States*. London: Andre Deutsch, 1956.

Matthews, Sallie Reynolds. *Interwoven, A Pioneer Chronicle*. Austin: University of Texas Press, 1958.

McConnell, H. H. *Five Years a Cavalryman*. Jacksboro: J. N. Rogers and Co., Printers, 1869.

McDowell, Catherine, editor. *Now You Hear My Horn, the Journal of James W. Nichols*. Austin: University of Texas Press, 1967.

Minge, Ward Alan. *Acoma: Pueblo in the Sky*. Albuquerque: University of New Mexico Press, 1976.

Moore, John M. *Life and I, or Sketches and Comments*. Nashville: Parthenon Press, 1948.

Moquin, Wayne, editor. *A Documentary History of the Mexican Americans*. New York: Praeger, 1971.

Mr. Speaker. (Excerpts from the Congressional Record Proceedings and Debates of the 82nd Congress, First Session, Wednesday, January 31, 1951.) Washington, D.C.: Government Printing Office, 1952.

Nance, Joseph. *Attack and Counterattack*. Austin: University of Texas Press, 1964.

Nance, Joseph. *After San Jacinto: The Texas-Mexican Frontier, 1836-1841*. Austin: University of Texas Press, 1963.

Neff, Pat M. *The Battles of Peace*. Fort Worth: Pioneer Publishing Co., 1925.

Nye, Wilbur. *Carbine and Lance*. Norman: University of Oklahoma Press, 1942.

O'Brien, H. V., Jr. *The Story of Old Rip*. Cisco, Texas: Longhorn Press, 1965.

Olmstead, F. L. *A Journey Through Texas*. Austin: University of Texas Press, 1978.

Paine, Albert. *Captain Bill McDonald, Texas Rangers*. New York: J. J. Little and Ives, Co., 1909.

Parsons, Elsie. *The Pueblo of Isleta*. Albuquerque: University of Albuquerque and Calvin-Horn Publisher, Inc., 1974.

Pershing, John J. *My Experiences in the World War*. London: Hodder and Stoughton, 1931.

Putnam, Wyvonne. *Navarro County History*. Quanah, Texas: Nortex Press, 1975.

Savage, W. Sherman. *Blacks in the West*. Westport, Connecticut: Greenwood Press, 1976.

Scobee, Barry. *The Story of Fort Davis, Jeff Davis County and the Davis Mountains*. Fort Davis: Marvin Hunter, Jr., 1936.

Scully, Vincent. *Pueblo, Mountain, Village, Dance*. New York: The Viking Press, 1972.

Seibel, Clifford W. *Helium, Child of the Sun*. Lawrence, Kansas: The University of Kansas Press, 1968.

Seymour, Charles. *The Intimate Papers of Colonel House*. Cambridge: Houghton-Mifflin Co., 1926.

Sibley, Marilyn, editor. *Samuel H. Walker's Account of the Mier Expedition*. Austin: Texas State Historical Association, 1978.

Stapp, William S. *The Prisoners of Perote*. Austin: University of Texas Press, 1977.

Stillman, Chauncey D. *Charles Stillman, 1810-1875*. New York: By the author, 1956.

Taylor, T. U. *Fifty Years on Forty Acres*. Austin: Alec Book Co., 1938.

Vandiver, Frank. *Black Jack*. College Station: Texas A & M Press, 1977.

Wallace, Ernest. *Ranald S. Mackenzie on the Texas Frontier*. Lubbock: West Texas Museum Assn., 1964.

Waller, John L. *Colossal Hamilton of Texas, A Biography of Andrew Jackson Hamilton*. El Paso: Texas Western Press, 1968.

Waugh, Julia Nott. *Castro-ville and Henri Castro, Empresario*. San Antonio: Standard Printing Co., 1934.

Webb, Walter P. *The Texas Rangers*. Austin: University of Texas Press, 1965.

White, Dabney and Richardson, T. C. *East Texas, Its History and Its Makers*. New York: Lewis Historical Publishing Co., 1940.

Williams, Annie Lee, *History of Wharton County*. Austin: Von Boeckmann-Jones Co., 1964.

Wooten, Dudley G., editor. *A Comprehensive History of Texas*. Dallas: William G. Scarff Co., 1898.

Magazines and Journals

Appleby, J. Gavin and Pierquet, Patrick. "T. V. Munson, American Grape Hybridizer." *American Wine Society Journal* (Spring, 1975).

Buckley, Eleanor. "The Aguayo Expedition into Texas and Louisiana, 1719-1722." *Quarterly of the Texas State Historical Association*, XV, No. 1 (July, 1911).

Carroll, H. Bailey. "The Texan Santa Fe Trail." *Panhandle-Plains Historical Review*, XXIV (1951).

Cox, Issac. "The Louisiana-Texas Frontier." *Quarterly of the Texas State Historical Association*, X, No. 1 (July, 1906).

Crimmins, M. L. "Colonel J. K. F. Mansfield's Report on the Inspection of the Department of Texas in 1856." *The Southwestern Historical Quarterly*, XLII, No. 2 (October, 1938).

Cullinane, Daniel B. "General B. H. Grierson, Indian Fighter." *Password*, IV (November 4, 1959).

Curry, Terry. "The Texan Who Saved the Vineyards of France." *Texas Historian* (November, 1974).

Newspapers

Abilene Reporter-News, March 30, 1974.
Austin American, September 30, 1930 and October 4, 1930.
Corsicana Daily Sun, June 29, 1976.
Dallas News, July 1, 1928; July 14, 1928; September 6, 1931.
Fort Worth Star-Telegram, March 1, 1936.
Los Angeles Times, April 7, 1939.
Lubbock Evening Journal, July 21, 1953.
Monahans News, November 5, 1937; December 2, 1938; November 28, 1941; Ward County 80th Anniversary Edition, 1972.
Oakland Post and Inquirer, March 24, 1939.
Oakland Tribune, March 25, 1939.

Special Publications

Clifton, Mrs. Minnie D. *A History of the Bloys Camp Meeting*. Pamphlet published by Sul Ross State Teachers College, 1947.

Publications of Amarillo Convention and Visitors Board.

Unpublished Manuscripts

Barker, Bernice. "The Texan Expedition to the Rio Grande in 1842." M. A. thesis, University of Texas at Austin, 1929.

Boden, William C. "The History of Kelly Field and Its Impact on American Aviation, 1917 to 1926." M. A. thesis, St. Mary's University, 1967.

Brown, Maury Bright. "The Military Defenses of Texas and the Rio Grande Region about 1766." M. A. thesis, University of Texas at Austin, 1924.

Carroll, Horace Bailey. "The Route of the Texan Santa Fe Expedition." Ph. D. dissertation, University of Texas at Austin, 1935.

Clark, Doris. "Spanish Reaction to French Intrusion into Texas from Louisiana, 1754-1771." M. A. thesis, University of Texas at Austin, 1942.

Cowling, Annie. "The Civil War Trade of the Lower Rio Grande Valley." M. A. thesis, University of Texas at Austin, 1926.

Friend, Llerena. "The Life of Thomas Jefferson Chambers." M. A. thesis, University of Texas at Austin, 1928.

Gittinger, Theodore D. "A History of St. Louis Catholic Church of Castroville, Texas." M. A. thesis, Sam Houston State University, 1972.

Goldthorp, Audrey. "Castro's Colony." M. A. thesis, University of Texas at Austin, 1928.

Gray, Ronald Norman. "The Abortive State of West Texas." M. A. thesis, Texas Tech, 1969.

Gregory, Hiram Ford. "Eighteenth Century Caddoan Archaeology, A Study in Models and Interpretation." Ph. D. dissertation, Southern Methodist University, 1973.

Hancock, Walter Edgar. "The Career of General Antonio Lopez de Santa Anna (1794-1833)." Ph. D. dissertation, University of Texas at Austin, 1933.

Harry, Jewel Horace. "History of Chambers County." M. A. thesis, University of Texas at Austin, 1940.

Havins, T. R. "Noah T. Byars." Ph. D. dissertation, University of Texas at Austin, 1941.

Hays, Robert A. "Military Aviation Activities in Texas, World War I and II." M. A. thesis, University of Texas at Austin, 1963.

Hill, Watt Goodwin, Jr. "Texan Santa Fe Expedition of 1841: A Visionary Dream." M. A. thesis, St. Mary's University, 1965.

Jordan, Ruby. "History of Chambers County" unpublished manuscript, no date.

Ledlow, William. "History of Protestant Education, A Study of the Origin, Growth and Development of Educational Endeavors in Texas." Ph. D. dissertation, University of Texas at Austin, 1926.

Marcum, Richard T. "Fort Brown, Texas: The History of a Border Post." Ph. D. dissertation, Texas Tech, 1964.

McGraw, John Conger. "The Texas Constitution of 1866." Ph. D. dissertation, Texas Tech, 1959.

Mendenhall, Christian. "William J. Marsh, A Biography and Study of His Liturgical Music." M. A. thesis, University of Dallas, 1978.

Middleton, Harry F. "A Frontier Outpost: A History of Fort Jesup." M. A. thesis, Louisiana State University, 1973.

Morris, Elizabeth Yates. "James Pinckney Henderson." M. A. thesis, University of Texas at Austin, 1931.

Munson, Regina. "Thomas Volney Munson, 1843-1912." unpublished manuscript, 1977.

Price, Margarett. "Judge Hayes' Discovery of the Willow Springs Massacre." unpublished manuscript, no date.

Reinhardt, Mrs. Kate Hamon. "The Public Career of Thomas Jefferson Green in Texas." M. A. thesis, University of Texas at Austin, 1939.

Roberts, Myrtle. "Roger Quarles Mills." M. A. thesis, University of Texas at Austin, 1929.

Rogers, Inez Dudley. "Not Made with Hands, The Story of the First Bloys Cowboy Camp Meeting, 1890." M. A. thesis, Sul Ross State College, 1952.

Selvaggi, Rossi L. "A History of Randolph Air Force Base." M. A. thesis, University of Texas at Austin, 1958.

Smith, Michael L. "The Role of Sam Houston in the Mier Expedition." M. A. thesis, Sam Houston State University, 1969.

Stearns, Joseph E. "Informal Relations Between the United States and Mexico, 1854-1877." M. A. thesis, University of Texas at Austin, 1965.

Stormont, Martha. "A Review of the Chambers Claim to the Capitol of Texas." M. A. thesis, Austin College, 1934.

Interviews

Bailey, Judge Scott, Eastland, Texas. Interview with author, January 27, 1976.

Dabney, F. James, Eastland, Texas. Interview with author, January 27, 1976.

Golden, James, Eastland, Texas. Interview with author, June 3, 1975.

Gray, Joe, Eastland, Texas. Interview with author, January 27, 1976.

Justin, Enid, Nocona, Texas. Interview with author, March 19, 1977.
Morrison, Ernest, Van Alstyne, Texas. Interview with author, May 11, 1978.

Letters and Maps

Coursey, Clark. *Courthouses of Texas*. Brownwood: Banner Printing Co., 1962.
McPherson, Dr. Clint. Lubbock, Texas. Letter to author, January 18, 1977.

Notes

1. The Settlement of Texas....Benavides; Castañeda; Horgan; Forrest; Hackett and Shelby; Moquin; Domínguez; Parson; Carter; Hodges.
2. For Half a Century....Hardin; Bancroft; Bolton; Buckley; Cox; Brown; de Mézières; Castañeda.
3. Zachary Taylor Founded....Hamilton; Henry; Grant; Gray.
4. T. J. Chambers owned....Friend; Stormont; Harry; Jordan.
5. Jack Hays was....Greer; Barton; Hunter; Webb; Nichols.
6. The Santa Fe Pioneers....Falconer; Loomis; Hill; Kendall; Carroll; Bell.
7. Somervell went in Pursuit....Stapp; Green; Bell; Barker; Reinhardt; Day; Smith; Nance.
8. The Mier Prisoners were....Bell; Barker; Green; Smith; Reinhardt; Day; Stapp; Sibley.
9. Navarro was....Dawson; Chabot; Grant; Ford; Green; Loomis; Nichols; Kendall.
10. Noah T. Byars organized....*Corsicana Daily Sun*; Havins; Putnam; Lockhart.
11. Alsatians settled....Dubuis; Gittinger; Finck; Goldthorp; Brown; Olmsted; Waugh.
12. The Army of Occupation moved....Henry; Grant; Lea; Hamilton.
13. Fort Brown was....Grant; Marcum; Hamilton; Waller; Chatfield.
14. American Blood was....Marcum; Hamilton; Henry; Wooten; Chatfield.
15. Taylor Prevailed....Hamilton; Henry; Grant; Cowling.
16. Charles Stillman Founded....Stillman; Lord; Chatfield.
17. Juan Cortina Captured....Maxey; Marcum; Ford; Cowling; Stearns; Chatfield.
18. Boehm Led....Carter.
19. The Fourth Cavalry Invaded....Carter; Wallace; La Torre; Gibson.
20. Grierson Commanded....Millet; Nye; Cullinane; Leckie; McConnell.
21. Uncle Charlie Carlton ran....Hay; Taylor; Ledlow; Hodge.
22. "80 John" Wallace was....Branch; Hendrix; Savage; Fowler.
23. T. V. Munson Received....Johnson; Munson; Curry; Hedrick; Castañeda; McPherson; Davis and Grobe.
24. Gorgas Began....Gorgas and Hendrick; Gibson; Gorgas.
25. Bloys Held a Camp Meeting....Clifton; Evans.
26. The Rope-Walker Died....Putnam; *Corsicana Daily Sun*.
27. The Monahans Sandhills were....*The Monahans News; A History of Ward County, Texas*; Foreman; Johnston; Price.
28. "The Eyes of Texas" was....Taylor; Benet; *Dallas News*; Morrison.
29. An Englishman wrote....Neff; Mendhall; *Dallas News; Fort Worth Star-Telegram*.
30. Bill McDonald was....Seymour; Paine; Webb.
31. American Military Aviation....Boden; Pershing; Vandiver; Foulois and Glines; Chandler and Lahm.
32. Cadet Brooks Died....Boden; Hays.
33. Randolph Field was....Selvaggi; Hays; Foulois and Glines.
34. Eastland's Old Rip Slept....House; *Dallas News; Austin American*; Bailey; Dabney; Gray; Golden; *Abilene Reporter-News; Lubbock Evening Journal*; O'Brien; Cox.
35. Enid Justin Sponsored....Justin; *Los Angeles Times; Oakland Tribune, Oakland Post and Inquirer*.
36. Amarillo is the....Seibel; Brendt; Lipper; Koelling and Balazik.

Index